super-cute
COOKIES

super-cute
COOKIES

35 easy to make and decorate cookie projects

chloe coker

CICO BOOKS

LONDON NEW YORK

For Jon, cookie taster extraordinaire

Published in 2011 by CICO Books
An imprint of Ryland Peters & Small Ltd
20-21 Jockey's Fields   519 Broadway, 5th Floor
London WC1R 4BW   New York, NY 10012

www.cicobooks.com

10 9 8 7 6 5 4 3 2 1

A CIP catalog record for this book is available from the Library
of Congress and the British Library.

ISBN: 978 1 907563 73 7

Printed in China

Editor: Alison Bolus
Design, styling, and art direction: Luis Peral-Aranda
Photographer: Martin Norris

Note
Standard level spoon measurements are used in all recipes,
unless otherwise stated:
1 tablespoon = one 15ml spoon
1 teaspoon = one 5ml spoon
Both imperial and metric measurements have been given.
Use one set of measurements only and not a mixture of both.
Eggs should be extra large (large) unless otherwise stated.
This book contains recipes made with raw eggs. It is prudent
for more vulnerable people, such as pregnant and nursing
mothers, babies and young children, invalids and the elderly,
to avoid uncooked dishes made with eggs. Some of the
recipes also contain nuts and should not be consumed by
anyone with a nut allergy.

contents

introduction

Many of my earliest and happiest memories are of standing on a chair in the kitchen learning how to cook. Although, over the years, the recipes have become more complex, the enjoyment remains the same—a love of all things homemade, the comforting association of food and family, and a sense of nostalgia for long afternoons in the kitchen. It is with this sentiment that I have approached this book, detailing delicious, homemade gifts for special occasions, projects that you can make with children, old-fashioned holiday baking, and vintage-style biscuits for weddings and parties.

Whether you are a first-time baker or an experienced cook, a busy parent or someone with time to bake, this book contains lots of achievable projects for many different occasions. And whether you choose something that involves helping little fingers to make a messy cookie or creating something beautiful and complicated, the most important thing is that you enjoy making it and people enjoy eating it.

Iced cookies are a great starting point for a first-time baker and a fun-to-make addition to an experienced repertoire: they are delicious and easy to make, the ingredients are inexpensive, the dough will keep in the refrigerator or can be frozen, they will keep for a long time in an airtight container and, most importantly, there are endless ways to decorate them.

From my own experience, I know that you may be so keen to get on to the fun stuff that you do not read the techniques section in detail—only coming back to it later if things haven't turned out quite how you expected. To try to avoid this, I have kept the techniques in the following section as brief as possible, including a few tasty recipes and some helpful hints and tips, so try to read it first. If you don't have time to read everything, look at the baking tips on pp.8–9 and the icing techniques on pp.16–21. It is a good idea to follow the recipes and measure accurately to start with, then, once you are happy, try experimenting with your own ideas.

I love teaching people to cook, and there is nothing more satisfying than seeing someone leave a class with something they did not think they could make at the beginning of the session. All the projects in this book are achievable with a bit of practice, and many of them are much easier to make than you may initially think. Just relax and enjoy yourself. Start with one of the simpler projects and build up your skills and confidence. Ideally, give all the projects a try, and don't worry if your cookies aren't perfect the first time around—you are likely to be the only person to notice. And, even if they don't work out exactly as planned, they will still taste great.

I hope you enjoy reading this book as much as I have enjoyed writing it. If you flick through it and are inspired to make something, then I will have achieved my aim. You probably already have the ingredients you need, so why not give it a go?

planning your cookies

Before you begin baking, think about a few practicalities: how many cookies you need to make, how much time you are likely to need, how difficult the design is, and whether you have all the necessary ingredients and equipment.

Start with the Bunting (p.34), Balloons (p.38), or many of the children's and holiday projects in chapters 2 and 3 if you are new to cookie making or would like to bake with your family. Move onto Afternoon Tea (p.26), Tulips and Butterfly (p.46), Fancy Hats (p.108), and Contemporary Flowers (p.112) to practice new skills and extend your repertoire. If you have made cookies before, you might like to try the Summer Daisies (p.40), Bridal Henna (p.102), Broderie Anglaise (p.104), or French Hearts (p.114). These projects might require more specialist decorating equipment and are a bit more challenging.

With some practice and confidence, all of the cookie collections in this book are achievable, and hopefully you will find that many of them are easier to complete than they may look. The most important thing is that you enjoy making them and that the end result tastes good.

designing your own cookies

You may also want to use the techniques and ideas in this book to create your own cookies. As described on p.11, you can design your own cookies and make your own templates and cutters. When designing a project, it is often helpful to draw out your cookie designs before you start so that you know exactly what you are going to do and you can have all your icing prepared before you begin. I tend to stick to between two and four colors and three or four variations on a design. This gives enough interest while making sure that the batch of cookies all look good together.

being organized

Try to be organized and have everything prepared before you begin icing your cookies so that you don't have to keep stopping to make up icing or fetch decorations. Work in a clear and organized area and move your cookies somewhere out of reach to dry. I can't tell you how many cookies I have ruined by knocking them when they are still drying. Finally, remember to relax and enjoy making your cookies.

enjoy!

You will usually be the only person who notices any flaws or mistakes in your cookies. Everyone else will be wowed by them, especially if they are lucky enough to receive them as a gift. And if anything does go really wrong when decorating them, the cookies will still taste good, so you can enjoy eating them while you make another batch!

succesful cookies

There is nothing more satisfying than taking a perfect tray of wonderful smelling, freshly baked cookies out of the oven. And nothing so disappointing as opening the oven door to find that, after all your hard work, they have not turned out as you had hoped. There are lots of simple techniques that you can follow to help ensure that you bake professional-looking cookies every time. It is also important to get to know your recipes and your oven. All kitchens and ovens are different, and the surrounding environment will also have an impact on your baking. The more you make the recipes, the easier it is to perfect them. Also, remember that icing will cover any number of lumps and bumps, plus, even if the cookies don't look perfect, they will still taste good!

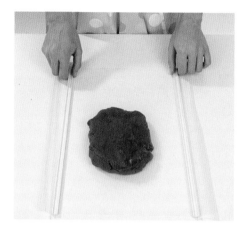

follow the recipes

To begin with, follow the recipes to the letter. Unlike some areas of cooking, where weights and measures don't matter too much, baking is all about ratios. It is important to measure accurately, whether you are measuring by volume or by weight. (If the latter, you will find that a digital scale is best for accuracy.) Also, follow the recipe steps carefully. As you become more confident, you can adjust recipes to suit your tastes or even make up your own. If you do this, think about what the ingredients are doing in the recipe and how the changes that you make will affect the end result. For example, if you are adding extra dry ingredients, you will probably want to reduce the amount of flour in the recipe to keep a balance. Butter and egg yolk add richness to a recipe, but can also make cookies greasy if you add too much. Nuts are also greasy, so you might want to reduce the amount of fat used in a recipe if you are increasing the nut content.

choose good-quality ingredients

One of the great things about cookies is that the ingredients are usually inexpensive and you probably already have many of them in your storecupboard. As a general rule, use the best ingredients that you can afford. This does not mean that you cannot make lovely cookies with basic ingredients, but I think that good-quality ingredients do make a difference, especially when it comes to butter, eggs, and vanilla. I like to use organic, free-range eggs. I use unsalted butter, so that I can control the amount of salt that goes into a recipe. When it comes to vanilla flavoring, I prefer to use vanilla extract rather than vanilla essence, and like to use vanilla bean paste if I have it: although more expensive than vanilla extract, it is stronger and has a lovely flavor.

follow these good-baking rules

• Take your dough out of the refrigerator about 10 minutes before you are ready to use it so that it is firm but not too hard to roll. I like to roll dough between two sheets of silicon or parchment paper, as it stops the dough sticking to the rolling pin. It also means that you don't need to flour your countertop (work surface), which dries out the dough.

• Use marzipan spacers as rolling guides on either side of the dough to ensure that it is flat and even. These spacers can be bought from cook and craft stores. As you roll, your rolling pin will eventually hit the rolling guides, which will stop you rolling the dough any thinner. Alternatively, use two new, clean strips of wood, about ¼in (5mm) thick, which you can buy from your local hardware store.

• Try not to handle your dough too much. Once you have rolled out your dough, cut out as many cookies as you can from it using a cutter or template—the best cookies will come from the first roll of dough. Scrunch up any remaining dough and re-roll it until you have used it all. If the dough becomes sticky or greasy looking, put it in the refrigerator for a few minutes to cool it down a little. If you have enough dough, it is always good to make a few spare cookies to account for breakages or just to practice on.

• Once you have cut out your cookies, transfer them to a cookie (baking) sheet lined with parchment paper using a palette knife, as this will stop the cookies sticking and will

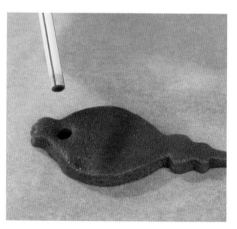

make it easier to transfer them from a hot cookie sheet to a cooling rack. Space your cookies out on the cookie sheet, leaving 1in (2.5cm) between each cookie, as they will spread slightly in the oven. Try to put cookies of the same size on the same sheet, as they are likely to require the same amount of time in the oven.

• If you would like to hang up your cookies when they are finished, make a hole in each one at this stage, before you bake them. A drinking straw is a good tool for a making a hole. Twist the drinking straw down through the dough and then lift out, leaving a hole.

• Put the cookies in the refrigerator until they are firm to the touch (usually about 30 minutes). This is very important, as it will help them to hold their shape in the oven.

• Once the cookies are firm, bake them in the oven following the recommended time in the recipe. Unless you have a convection (fan) oven, you may need to turn the tray halfway through baking to make sure the cookies bake evenly. If you have more than one tray in the oven, remember that the bottom tray will take longer to cook, so swap the trays around halfway through baking. Cookies will usually develop a cookie-like smell and be just starting to brown on the edges when they are cooked.

cooling

Note that the cookies will still be soft to the touch when they are cooked but will crisp up as they cool, so be careful when transferring them to a cooling rack: either lift them and the parchment paper off as a whole or use a palette knife to transfer them individually. Make sure you cool the cookies on a cooling rack rather than leaving them on the cookie sheet, as otherwise they will go soggy.

storing

One of the great things about cookies is that the dough lasts a long time and can be made ahead. Unbaked cookie dough will keep for a couple of days in the refrigerator or can be frozen for a month or two. It is also fine to freeze baked cookies, although I prefer to cut out the cookies and freeze them unbaked. Simply stack them between sheets of parchment paper in an airtight lidded box and store in the freezer until you need them. You can then take them out of the freezer and bake them from frozen, which will make your kitchen smell lovely and will give your cookies a lovely freshly baked taste. Baked cookies will also keep in an airtight container for a couple of weeks. If they lose their freshness, simply refresh them (even if they have been iced) by putting them in the oven on its lowest setting for 20 minutes (see p.23).

(see p.23)

troubleshooting tips

Why has the dough become sticky and greasy while I'm cutting out the cookies?
It has become too warm, either because it is in a warm kitchen or because it has been handled a lot. Put it back in the refrigerator for 10 minutes and wait for it to firm up a little before you carry on cutting.

Why have my cookies spread and lost their shape in the oven?
Once you have cut out your cookies, make sure you chill them in the refrigerator until they are firm (usually around 30 minutes) before you bake them. This helps them to keep their shape.

How can I prevent my cookies from being uneven when I roll them?
Use marzipan spacers or two clean strips of wood as rolling guides to make sure the dough is rolled to an even thickness.

How can I stop my dough sticking to my rolling pin and countertop?
Roll it between two sheets of silicon or parchment paper. Put very sticky dough in the refrigerator for 10 minutes to firm up.

Why are my cookies a bit soggy?
Make sure that you bake your cookies for sufficient time, then transfer them to a cooling rack to cool, and finally store them in an airtight container. Remember that you can refresh them in a low oven to give them a freshly baked feel (see p.23).

Why has the icing overflowed when I put it on the cookie?
There may have been a gap or two in the outline of the cookie. Alternatively, you may have used too much icing or icing that is too runny. Try using a slightly thicker consistency next time.

equipment

One of the great things about making cookies is that you are already likely to have most of the key equipment that you will need to make a number of the ideas in this book. Over time, you can collect more equipment to help perfect your baking and develop your skills.

Key equipment: rolling pin; flat cookie (baking) sheets rather than the ones with raised edges; cookie cutters or templates (see below); parchment paper; toothpicks (cocktail sticks); scissors; cooling rack; dressmaking pins; a knife

Specialist equipment: plunger cutters; tappit cutters; edible glitter; silver or gold powder; flower paste; gel food colorings; flower cutters; embossing tools; modeling tools

Ideal equipment: icing tips (nozzles) in fine, medium, and thick sizes; squeezy bottles; marzipan spacers or ¼in (5mm) thick strips of wood; nonstick rolling pin; soft paintbrushes; edible glue; sprinkles; piping bags

DIY equipment

You might be surprised to know that you can make some of the equipment yourself, such as templates, cookie cutters, and piping bags, so keeping the costs down and also allowing your cookies to be truly individual.

templates

Where I have used my own templates for cookies, these can be found on pp.122–6. Trace the templates onto tracing paper and transfer them onto cardstock (cardboard) or acetate, which will make fairly sturdy shapes to cut around. Roll out your dough, place the template on top, and cut around it with a knife. Try to cut downward rather than dragging your knife through the dough. Once you have cut out each cookie, you may want to smooth the edges with your fingers.

You can also draw your own templates. If you are making your own templates, remember that simple shapes are easier to cut out and less likely to break. You can always pipe a more detailed outline onto the cookie, but try to keep the actual cookie shape as simple as possible. For example, the octopus template on p.126 does not include each individual tentacle; instead, the outline has been simplified and the individual tentacles are simply piped onto the cookie, to great effect.

cookie cutters

Although the majority of the projects in this book are made with cutters from cook and craft stores (see suppliers, p.128), for which you can substitute your own cutters, adapting the design to fit, you can also buy easy-to-use kits to make your own cookie cutters, should you want a specific shape. (Whilst templates are fine for making small batches of bespoke cookies, making your own cutters for large or repeat batches of cookies makes sense.)

2 Draw out a template for your cutter. Put this on the shaping board and use it as a guide for forming the cutter. Then use the corner or curved attachments to bend the aluminum into the required shape.

1 Although kits may vary, they are likely to include a shaping board, strips of aluminum, and some special tape to stick the cutter together. Follow the manufacturers' instructions carefully.

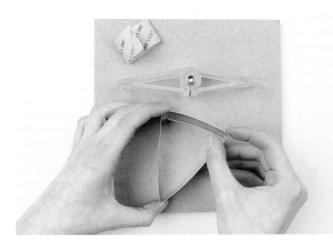

3 Make sure that the ends of your cutter overlap,

4 Stick them together with the tape. Leave the glue to dry completely before using the cutter.

piping bags

I either use disposable plastic piping bags (see suppliers, p.128) or make my own from parchment paper, as shown here.

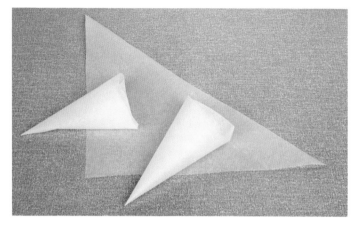

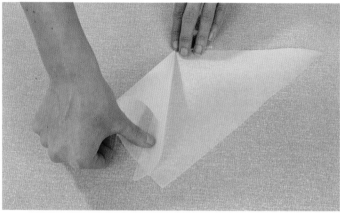

1 To make a paper piping bag, cut a large square of parchment paper, then cut it in half across the diagonal to make a triangle.

2 Put your finger in the center of the long side—this is where the tip of the piping bag will be. Take one of the corners of the piping bag and roll it into the middle to make a cone in one half of the triangle.

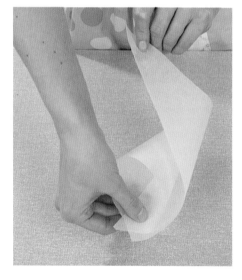

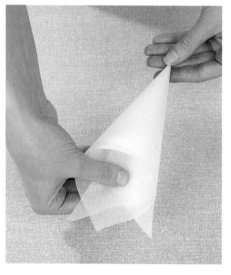

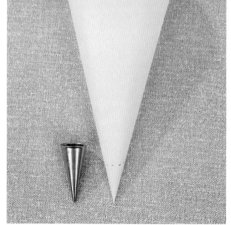

3 Wrap the other half of the triangle around the cone.

4 All three corners of the triangle should end up at the top of the bag. Fold all of the corners into the cone to secure it.

5 Once you have made the piping bag, you can either snip the end off or you can put an icing tip (nozzle) in it. If you are using an icing tip, the end of the bag should come about halfway down the tip. To ensure this, hold the tip against the bag and cut the end of the bag off at the appropriate point.

cookie recipes

vanilla cookie dough

This dough makes lovely crumbly, buttery cookies. It is delicious as it is but is also very versatile, as it can easily be altered to incorporate lots of different flavors (see below).

2½ cups (250g) all-purpose (plain) flour
1¼ cups (125g) self-rising (self-raising) flour
pinch of salt
2 sticks (250g) sweet (unsalted) butter, at room temperature
⅔ cup (125g) unrefined superfine (golden caster sugar)
1 egg yolk
1 tsp vanilla extract

1 Sift the flours and salt into a mixing bowl and set aside.
2 Cream the butter and sugar in another bowl until light and fluffy.
3 Beat in the egg yolk and vanilla extract until they are fully incorporated.
4 Finally, add the flours and mix everything together until all the flour is incorporated and the mixture forms a dough. Stop mixing as soon as the flour is incorporated, as you do not want to overwork the dough.
5 Put the dough in a sealable food bag and chill for at least 1 hour.
6 Referring to the good-baking rules on p.8, roll out the cookie dough and cut out the cookies. Place the cookies on a lined cookie (baking) sheet and chill for 30 minutes. Meanwhile, preheat the oven to 400°F/200°C/Gas 6 (convection/fan 350°F/180°C).
7 Bake for 12–16 minutes until the cookies are golden and smell baked.

VARIATIONS

Lemon: Add the finely grated rind/zest of 1 lemon to the mixture when you add the egg yolk and vanilla extract.

Orange and almond: Add the finely grated rind/zest of 1 orange to the mixture when you add the egg yolk and vanilla extract. Replace 1¼ cups (125g) of the flour with 1½ cups (125g) of ground almonds.

Almond: Replace the vanilla extract with 1 teaspoon of almond essence, and 1¼ cups (125g) of the flour with 1½ cups (125g) of ground almonds.

Chocolate: Replace ½ cup (60g) of the flour with ½ cup (60g) of unsweetened cocoa powder. This recipe makes a lovely dark chocolate cookie that works well with the sweetness of the icing. If you prefer a sweeter cookie, add another tablespoon of sugar.

Chocolate-orange: Add the finely grated rind/zest of an orange to the chocolate variation above.

Lavender: Add 1 tablespoon of dried, edible lavender, which can be bought from many health food and specialist cook stores.

gingerbread cookie dough

Gingerbread is a great cookie dough, because it makes the house smell wonderful and keeps really well, both baked and unbaked. It is also an easy recipe to personalize. This recipe makes a gently spiced cookie with a hint of citrus, but you can change the quantities of spices to suit your tastes and even add a pinch of ground pepper for some extra zing.

1 stick (125g) unsalted butter
½ cup (100g) dark soft brown sugar
2 tbsp water
2 tbsp light corn (golden) syrup
1 tbsp molasses (treacle)
2½ cups (250g) all-purpose (plain) flour
½ tsp baking soda (bicarbonate of soda)
1 cup (100g) self-rising (self-raising) flour
1 tbsp ground ginger
2 tsp ground cinnamon
2 tsp apple pie spice (mixed spice)
finely grated rind/zest of 1 orange or lemon (optional)

1 Put the butter, sugar, water, syrup, and molasses in a heavy-based saucepan and melt over a low heat, stirring occasionally. Remove from the heat and leave to cool for a few minutes.
2 Meanwhile, sift the flours, baking soda, and all the spices together into a large bowl, and add the citrus rind.
3 Make a well in the middle of the dry ingredients and pour in the melted mixture. Gently stir in the flour, so that there are no lumps, until the mixture comes together to form a soft dough.
4 Put the dough in a sealable food bag and leave in the refrigerator for at least 1 hour.
5 Referring to the good-baking rules on p.8, roll out the cookie dough and cut out the cookies. Place the cookies on a lined cookie (baking) sheet and chill for 30 minutes. Meanwhile, preheat the oven to 400°F/200°C/ Gas 6 (convection/fan 350°F/180°C).
6 Bake for 8–12 minutes until the cookies are golden and smell baked.

When grating orange or lemon rind/zest, try to grate it as finely as possible and avoid grating the white pith, as this is what gives the fruit its bitter taste.

lemon spice cookie dough

These cookies are a milder version of the gingerbread cookies but still have a lovely festive smell. They are perfect for children or for adults who prefer a milder biscuit.

1 stick (125g) unsalted butter
½ cup (100g) dark soft brown sugar
2 tbsp freshly squeezed lemon juice
2 tbsp light corn (golden) syrup
1 tbsp clear honey
2½ cups (250g) all-purpose (plain) flour
1 cup (100g) self-rising (self-raising) flour
½ tsp baking soda (bicarbonate of soda)
1 tbsp apple pie spice (mixed spice)
finely grated rind/zest of 1 lemon

1 Put the butter, sugar, lemon juice, syrup, and honey in a heavy-based saucepan and melt over a low heat, stirring occasionally. Remove from the heat and leave to cool for a few minutes.
2 Meanwhile, sift the flours, baking soda, and apple pie spice (mixed spice) together into a large bowl, and add the lemon rind.
3 Make a well in the middle of the dry ingredients and pour in the melted mixture. Gently stir in the flour so that there are no lumps until the mixture comes together to form a soft dough.
4 Put the dough in a sealable food bag and leave in the refrigerator for at least 1 hour.
5 Referring to the good-baking rules on p.8, roll out the cookie dough and cut out the cookies. Place the cookies on a lined cookie (baking) sheet and chill for 30 minutes. Meanwhile, preheat the oven to 400°F/200°C/Gas 6 (convection/fan 350°F/180°C).
6 Bake for 8–12 minutes until the cookies are golden and smell baked.

To stop light corn syrup sticking to your spoon and making a mess, rinse the spoon in hot water before putting it into the syrup. It should then glide off your spoon into the bowl.

vanilla nut cookie dough

These lovely nutty cookies are adapted from my friend Sophie's grandmother's cookie recipe. They hold their shape well and have a really nice texture and flavor. I think they work particularly well with pecan nuts or toasted hazelnuts.

½ cup (100g) nuts of your choice
1 stick (115g) chilled unsalted butter, diced
2½ cups (250g) all-purpose (plain) flour
1 heaped cup (100g) ground almonds
½ cup (100g) light brown sugar
1 extra large (large) egg
2 tbsp light corn (golden) syrup
1 tsp vanilla extract

1 Grind the nuts in a food processor or blender or put them in a bag and crush them with a rolling pin.
2 Rub the butter into the flour using the tips of your fingers, or use a food processor. Then stir in all the ground nuts and the sugar.
3 Make a well in the center of the mixture and add the egg, syrup, and vanilla extract. Mix everything together to form a stiff dough.
4 Put the dough in a sealable food bag and leave in the refrigerator for at least 1 hour.
5 Referring to the good-baking rules on p.8, roll out the cookie dough and cut out the cookies. Place the cookies on a lined cookie (baking) sheet and chill for 30 minutes. Meanwhile, preheat the oven to 400°F/200°C/Gas 6 (convection/fan 350°F/180°C).
6 Bake for 8–12 minutes until the cookies are golden and smell baked. These cookies take on color very quickly, so watch them carefully when they are in the oven.

For a lovely toasted flavor, put the whole nuts in a roasting tin and roast in the oven for 10 minutes at 400°F/200°C/Gas 6 (convection/fan 350°F/180°C), before grinding.

VARIATION

Cookie lollipops

These unusual cookies are fantastic for children's parties or weddings or for making bunches of cookie flowers. Cookie lollipop sticks are widely available in cook or craft stores.

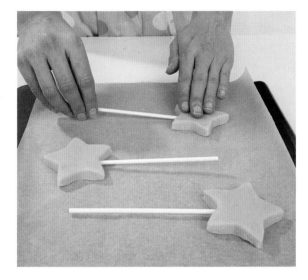

1 Roll your cookie dough slightly thicker (⅜in/8–10mm) than usual. Cut out your cookies in the normal way, using a cutter or template. With one hand, gently twist the lollipop stick into the bottom of the cookie. Place the fingers of your other hand on the top of the cookie so that you can feel where the stick is. Keep twisting the stick until it is at least two-thirds of the way up the cookie. Don't worry if the stick breaks through the bottom of the cookie, as you will be attaching more dough.

2 Carefully turn the cookie over. Roll a small sausage of cookie dough and attach it to the bottom of the cookie where the stick is. This will strengthen the cookie and will disappear when it is baked. Bake and cool as usual.

royal icing

Royal icing is traditionally made with egg whites, but if you want to avoid using raw eggs, there are two options open to you (see below). Always make sure your mixing bowl is clean and grease free.

egg-white royal icing

2 extra large (large) egg whites
3¼ cups (450g) confectioners' (icing) sugar
2 tsp lemon juice

Put the egg white and lemon juice into a large, clean, grease-free bowl. Slowly add the confectioners' sugar, mixing it gently by hand or on a slow speed until it is incorporated. This will stop your kitchen being filled with clouds of sugar. You can then increase the speed to medium and beat the icing for 5–10 minutes until it turns bright white and glossy and holds its shape like a stiff meringue.

powdered egg-white royal icing

This is a general recipe, by way of a guide, but always follow the manufacturers' instructions, as they will vary.

2 tsp or 1 sachet powdered egg white
3 tbsp water
3 cups (400g) confectioners' (icing) sugar

1 In a small bowl, combine the egg white powder with 1 tablespoon of the water to make a paste. Add the remaining water gradually, mixing thoroughly to avoid any lumps. To make sure your icing is beautifully smooth, you may want to press the mixture through a sifter (sieve).
2 Place the egg white mixture in the bottom of a large, clean, grease-free bowl. Slowly add the confectioners' sugar, mixing it gently by hand or using a hand-held mixer on a slow speed, until it is incorporated. Then increase the speed to medium and beat the icing for about 5 minutes until it turns bright white and glossy and holds its shape like a stiff meringue.

royal icing powder

It is also possible to purchase ready-mixed royal icing powder. Follow the manufacturers' instructions, which usually say to add the recommended amount of water to the bottom of a clean, grease-free bowl and beat in the confectioners' (icing) sugar as above.

flavorings

Add one of these flavorings to a batch of royal icing for extra interest:

2 tsp lemon juice
½ tsp vanilla extract
½ tsp almond extract
½ tsp peppermint extract

making flooding icing

To flood your cookies, you need to thin the royal icing with a little water until it reaches the consistency of emulsion paint. It should be thin enough that it will spread when it goes onto the cookie but not too thin so that it runs off the edge. When you start out, it is best to err on the thicker side, as it is less likely to overflow. The exact amount of water that you need to add will depend on the day, the temperature of your kitchen, the weather, etc., so add teaspoon by teaspoon until you reach the correct consistency. Once you have iced a few cookies, you will know what to aim for.

making piping icing for outlining

Piping icing should have the consistency of a stiff meringue mixture—firm enough to hold its own shape but still soft enough to pipe. For the best results, make sure that all of your equipment is clean and grease free. Although traditionally egg whites are used to make royal icing, it is preferable to use an egg-white substitute to avoid the risk associated with eating raw eggs. Beat your icing for 5–10 minutes using electric beaters or an electric stand mixer until it reaches the consistency of a firm meringue and turns glossy.

Once you have made your icing, cover it with plastic wrap (cling film) or with a new, damp, disposable cloth (making sure the plastic wrap or cloth touches the surface of the icing to prevent it from forming a skin). Your icing will be at its best the day that it is made, but it can be kept in the refrigerator for a couple of days. If you are keeping it, do not color it until you are ready to use it, and give it a good mix before you use it. Squeezy bottles are an excellent alternative to piping bags: they are easy to control, are mess free, and do not dry out easily.

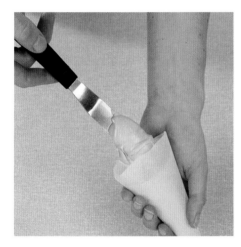

1 If you want to use it for piping straightaway, put some of the icing on a palette knife, and put the knife in the piping bag. Close the bag together with your fingers and then pull the palette knife out.

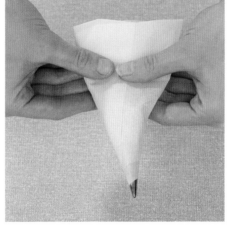

2 Work the icing down the bag with your fingers and fold down the top to close it.

3 When taking a break from icing, store your piping bags in a glass with damp kitchen paper in the bottom to stop them from drying out.

coloring icing

It is best to color your icing in one batch, before you divide it into piping and flooding icing. Although you can use supermarket-bought food colorings to dye your icing, I would recommend that you invest in some professional gel colorings if possible (see suppliers, p.128). They are available in a wide range of colors and, although they are more expensive than traditional food colorings, they are concentrated and therefore go a long way. To begin with, buy just a few basic colors, as one color can make any number of shades. To color your icing, put a small amount of coloring on the end of a toothpick (cocktail stick) and add it to the icing. Be cautious, as you can always add more if needed, and you may be surprised at how strong it is. Mix the color through thoroughly with a spoon.

covering cookies

There are two main ways to cover a cookie: flooding it with royal icing or covering it with rolled fondant (sugarpaste). Both methods produce lovely results and are often interchangeable, depending on your personal preference.

flooding with icing

With this method, the icing dries very hard to give the cookie a lovely smooth professional finish. It is a more complicated and time-consuming method than using rolled fondant, but it produces beautiful results. This is the method used by many professional cookie makers. Flooded cookies are made in two stages: first they are outlined with piping icing and then they are flooded with flooding icing. Both types of icing are made from the same basic royal icing, with the consistency adjusted to suit the purpose (see p.16). As a guide, you will need one-third of the icing in each flooded recipe to outline the cookies and the other two-thirds to flood them.

outlining cookies

When piping icing, make sure the top of the piping bag is tightly folded down so that the bag is taut. The pressure should be coming from the top of the bag, so squeeze the bag from the top, not the middle, using your dominant hand. You may want to use the fingers of your other hand to steady the bag. The purpose of the outline is to create a barrier to hold the flooding icing on the cookie. With your first few projects, you may want to use a wider tip (nozzle) (Wilton size 4) to make a thicker barrier so that the icing is less likely to overflow. As you get more confident, you will be able use a narrow tip (Wilton size 1–2), which gives a more subtle outline.

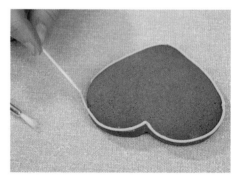

1 When outlining the cookie, pipe as close to the edge of the cookie as possible. Hold the bag at a 45-degree angle, apply even pressure, and move the bag steadily along the cookie.

2 For best results, lift the tip off the cookie and allow the icing to fall, rather than dragging the tip along the surface of the cookie.

3 Don't worry if it goes wrong: the icing will be fairly elastic and you will be able to move it with a toothpick (cocktail stick) or use a damp paintbrush to tidy your icing. Although the neater the better, don't worry if your outline is not perfect, provided there are no gaps in it. Once the cookie is flooded, you won't notice any minor imperfections. Leave the outline to dry for a few minutes before flooding the cookie (see opposite).

flooding cookies

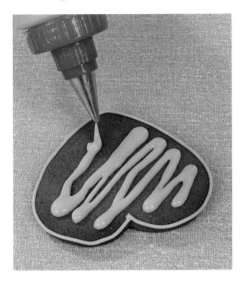 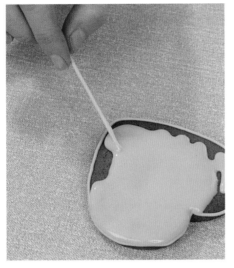 

1 Squeeze some icing onto the cookie, keeping it away from the edges. You want to squeeze enough icing onto the cookie so that it looks generously covered, but not so much that it overflows.

2 Use a toothpick (cocktail stick) to guide the icing so that it floods any gaps.

3 Once you have flooded the cookie, check the surface for any air bubbles and pop them with the toothpick. Note that if you start flooding your cookies and realize that the consistency is not quite right, it is better to stop and fix it rather than persevering, as the results will never be satisfactory.

special effects: wet-on-wet technique

 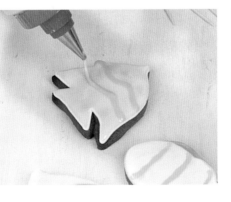 

To add polka dots to a flooded cookie, make up some flooding (or "wet") icing in another color. While the cookie is still wet, dot spots of wet icing onto the cookie.

For stripes, pipe a line of wet icing. The icing will sink in and dry flat.

For a marbled effect, pipe a line of wet icing and then pull a toothpick (cocktail stick) through it.

covering with rolled fondant

Rolled fondant (sugarpaste), which is also sold as ready-to-roll/roll out/rolled icing, is available in most cook and craft stores and many supermarkets. It is the icing that you would buy to cover your Christmas cake. It provides a very quick and easy way to decorate cookies and is ideal for children, as it is not as complicated as flooding cookies with royal icing. If the icing does not stick, and you have no edible glue, use a little corn syrup or sugar syrup made from dissolving sugar and warm water on a 1:1 ratio and brush over the cookies.

 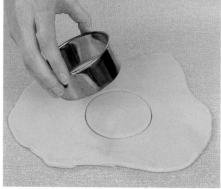 

1 Work the icing between your fingers until it is pliable. Try not to use your palms, as they will make the icing sticky. To color the icing, put some coloring on a toothpick (cocktail stick) and put it in the icing, then knead the icing until the color is fully blended with no streaks.

2 Roll the icing out on a countertop (work surface) dusted with confectioners' (icing) sugar to ⅛in (3mm) thick. Then cut out with the cookie cutter. If the icing is not too dry, it will stick to the cookie; alternatively, brush the cookie with edible glue using a damp brush.

3 Attach the icing to the cookie. If the cookie has spread a little in the oven, lightly roll over the icing to stretch it right to the edges of the cookie. Finally, run your finger around the edge of the icing to smooth it onto the cookie for a perfect finish.

special effects: polka dots and stripes

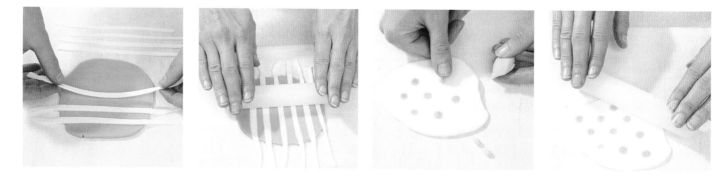

Polka-dot and striped rolled fondant (sugarpaste) look great on cookies. To make stripes, roll out some colored icing as normal. Then roll out some white icing to ⅛in (3mm) thick, cut it into thin strips and lay them over the colored icing. Note that the strips should be slightly narrower than the stripes you want, as the icing will be squashed, and so will spread when it is rolled. Gently roll over the strips with a rolling pin so that they become incorporated into the colored icing as stripes.

To make polka-dot icing, roll out some white icing as normal. Then roll some small balls of colored icing between your fingers and squash these down onto the white icing using your thumb. When all the balls are in place, gently roll over the icing to incorporate the dots.

decorating cookies

Once you have covered your cookies, finish them with fine detailing and gorgeous decorations to make them extra special. The projects in this book highlight some of the many techniques for finishing your cookies, from intricate piping to adding buttons, flowers, and glitter.

piping

Use the piping icing that you used to outline the cookie or make up fresh icing in different colors following the steps on pp.16–17. Piping icing can be used to re-outline the cookie for extra definition (see the chicks on p.90), to pipe intricate patterns onto the bridal henna cookies (p.102), or for adding extra detailing (such as on the Christmas trees on p.88). Remember to keep a fine damp paintbrush to hand when you are piping so that you can correct any mistakes.

scalloped borders

These look lovely on pretty cookies such as Baby Shoes and French Hearts (pp.32 and 114). Holding the tip (nozzle) above the cookie, carefully pipe a series of "U" shapes, letting the icing fall into place. You may want to draw the pattern onto some tracing or baking paper and practice before you pipe it on the cookie.

polka dots

These are great for adding a pattern to your cookies, such as on Broderie Anglaise and Baby Grows (pp.104 and 28) or for piping eyes onto creatures, such as the tropical fish in Under the Sea on p.70. Hold the tip (nozzle) near to the surface of the cookie and squeeze out a ball of icing. Stop squeezing and lift off. If there is a slight tail left on the dot when you lift off, smooth it down with a damp paintbrush.

hearts

To pipe a heart, as used on the Christmas Trees (p.88) and Baby Grows (p.28), pipe a "V" shape, applying more pressure at the beginning and end of the "V". You can smooth the heart shape with a damp paintbrush.

transferring designs

Simple graphic shapes and flowers, as used in Bridal Henna (p.102) and Contemporary Flowers (p.112), look fantastic on plain-iced cookies. To transfer a design to your cookie, follow the steps below.

1 Trace the relevant template from pp.122–4 onto some tracing paper.

2 Once you have traced the design, go over it with a clean dressmaking pin, pricking the paper every ⅛in (3mm). Pricking the pattern through like this before the template is resting on the cookie avoids pressing on the cookie when transferring the design, and so leaving unwanted dents on the icing. Place the traced design on the cookie and prick through all the holes that you have already made with the pin. When you lift the paper off, an imprint of the design will be left on the cookie.

3 Using a fine tip (nozzle) (Wilton size 1 or 1.5), pipe the design onto the cookie following the imprinted pattern.

using small cutters

Small cutters are fantastic for cutting out decorations from rolled fondant (sugarpaste). I particularly like plunger cutters, which are widely available from cook and craft stores (see suppliers, p.128). Simply roll out some icing to ⅛in (3mm) thick, cut out the shape, wiggle it a little bit to tidy the edges, then lift off. If you are using a plunger cutter, push down the plunger to eject the shape. To attach the shapes to the cookie, simply brush them with a little sugar syrup or edible glue to make them stick. Edible glue is available from most cook and craft shops. Alternatively, you can use a little water, corn syrup, or sugar syrup to stick rolled fondant to your cookies. To make sugar syrup, put equal amounts of sugar and water in a pan on a low heat until the sugar dissolves. Bring it to a boil and boil for one minute, then let it cool.

To make very fine decorations, buy flower paste, also known as petal paste (available from many cook and craft stores). This icing can be rolled very thin and dries very hard, making it ideal for delicate work. If you are using flower paste, make sure you cover it with plastic wrap (cling film) while you are not using it, as it dries out very quickly.

making buttons

Buttons look gorgeous on children's cookies, such as Baby Grows and Train Set (see pp.28 and 68).

1 To make a button, roll out some rolled fondant (sugarpaste) and cut a small circle using a round cutter. Using a smaller cutter, indent an inner circle, but do not push it all the way through.

2 Then, using a toothpick (cocktail stick), mark 2 or 4 holes in the center of the button.

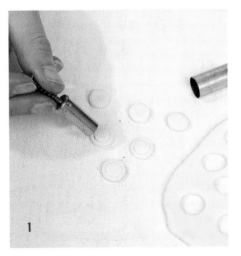

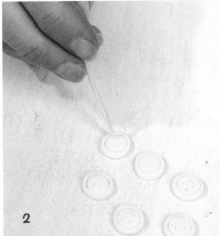

adding bows

Bows are another gorgeous decoration to add to cookies (see Polka-dot Presents, p.80, Christmas puddings, p.82, and Fancy Hats, p.108). The steps to make a bow are set out in detail in on p.80.

embossing

An embossed design is a great way to add a textured pattern to your cookies. Roll out some rolled fondant (sugarpaste) to ⅛in (3mm) thick and lightly push a cutter or embossing tool (see p.128 for stockists) into the icing (not all the way through). Lift off the cutter to leave a pattern.

adding sparkle

Add extra sparkle to your cookies by using gold or silver paint or glitter, as in A Girl's Best Friend (see p.100). You can buy edible gold and silver powders from many craft and cook stores. Simply mix a little powder with some clear alcohol to make a paint, then brush it onto the cookie once the icing has dried.

Alternatively, edible glitter and sprinkles look great on children's cookies and add some festive sparkle to holiday cookies. Put your cookies on some parchment paper and sprinkle the glitter or sprinkles over them. Shake off any excess onto the paper and pour it back into the container.

---

drying out and refreshing

If you are giving your cookies as gifts, leave them to dry completely, preferably overnight, before putting them in a container. Alternatively, you can dry out your cookies in a low oven: put your oven on its lowest setting and put the iced cookies in the oven on cookie (baking) sheets for around half an hour. You can also use this method to refresh your cookies if you have spent a couple of days making them or have kept them for a few days before giving them as a gift. This gives the cookies that freshly baked feel again and will not damage the icing, provided that the oven is not too hot.

chapter 1

celebrations and gifts

Make special occasions truly personal with these
gorgeous handmade gifts: with balloons and bunting
for birthdays and parties, cute baby grows for new
arrivals, cookie flowers for loved ones, and kitsch
cookies for vintage tea parties, this chapter contains
lots of beautiful one-off gift ideas.

afternoon tea

These kitsch cherry tea sets are inspired by colorful 1950s kitchenware. They are perfect for a tea party, a birthday gift, or Mother's Day.

YOU WILL NEED:
6 teacup cookies and
　　6 teapot cookies made
　　from a recipe on pp.13–14,
　　using cookie cutters
1 recipe light blue royal
　　icing (see pp.16–17)
¼ recipe each brown, red,
　　green, and white royal
　　icing

EQUIPMENT
teacup and teapot cookie
　　cutters
5 piping bags (see p.12) with
　　fine (1–2) tips (nozzles)
1 squeezy bottle or piping
　　bag with thick (4) tip
toothpick (cocktail stick)
soft paintbrush

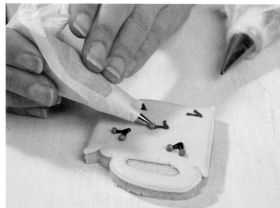

2 When the icing has dried, make the cherry stalks by piping "V" shapes in brown icing with another fine tip. Then pipe red dots at the end of the stalks for the cherries using another fine tip.

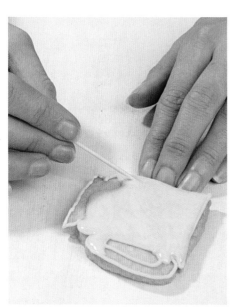

1 Outline and flood the cookies using a fine tip for the outline and a thick tip for the flooding, following the steps on pp.18–19.

3 To pipe the leaves, pipe a green dot and pull downward and away with the tip as you lift off. Then gently pull a damp paintbrush through the dot to make the leaf shape.

4 With white icing, pipe little polka dots and lines to mark the trim of the teacups. Repeat with the teapot cookies.

baby grows

These baby grows make a lovely gift for a new baby or a baby shower. Keep the base icing simple with plain pastels or cute polka dots, then add piped or rolled fondant detailing with ducks, hearts, flowers, and buttons.

YOU WILL NEED:
12 baby grow cookies made
    from a recipe on pp.13–14,
    using a cookie cutter
½ recipe white royal icing
    (see pp.16–17)
¼ recipe each yellow and
    pink or blue royal icing
confectioners' (icing) sugar,
    for dusting
3½oz (100g) rolled fondant
    (sugarpaste) (see p.20)
edible glue

EQUIPMENT
baby-grow cookie cutters
4 piping bags (see p.12) with
    fine (1–2) tips (nozzles)
4 squeezy bottles or piping
    bags with thick (4) tips
toothpicks (cocktail sticks)
rolling pin
soft paintbrush
small and medium round
    cutters

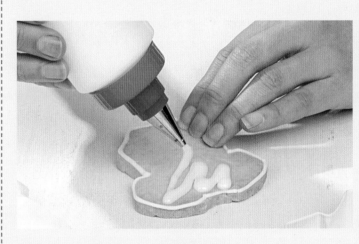

1 Outline and flood the cookies using a fine tip for the outline and a large tip for the flooding, following the steps on pp.18–19, with white, pink, or blue royal icing.

2 While the icing is still wet, add any polka dots by dotting yellow wet icing onto the flooded cookie, using the wet-on-wet technique (see p.19).

3 Using a fine tip, pipe the seams and edges, where relevant, onto the cookies.

4 For added detail, pipe hearts, dots, and flowers. To pipe a heart, pipe a "V" shape, putting more pressure at the start and end of the "V." Then flatten out the heart with a damp paintbrush.

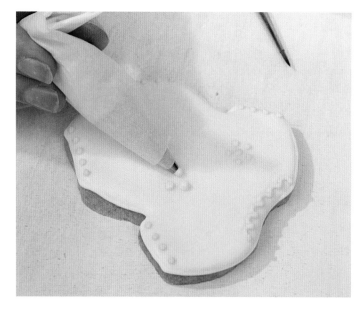

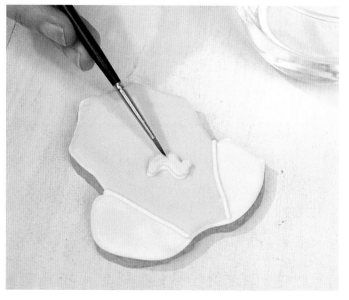

5 To pipe a dot of icing, put the tip near to the cookie and squeeze out a ball of icing. Release the pressure and then lift off. If the dot has a slight tail when lifted off, round it off with a damp paintbrush.

6 To pipe a duck, pipe the outline of the duck using a fine tip, then fill in the center with the same icing and smooth it with the paintbrush.

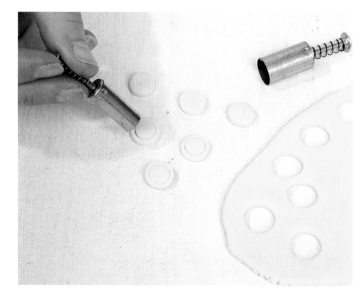

7 To make buttons, dust the countertop (work surface) with some confectioners' sugar and roll out the rolled fondant. Cut a circle with the larger of the 2 cutters. I have used plunger cutters for ease. Using the smaller cutter, indent an inner circle, but do not push right through.

8 Using a toothpick, mark 2 or 4 holes in the center of each button and attach it to the cookie with edible glue.

baby shoes

Present these cute cookies to proud new parents or to celebrate baby's first birthday. Make them dainty and girly with lacy edging and little flowers, or cool and kitsch for little boys with buttons, stars, and polka dots.

YOU WILL NEED:

12 baby shoe cookies made from a recipe on pp.13–14, using a cookie cutter

½ recipe pink or blue royal icing (see pp.16–17)

¼ recipe white royal icing

¼ recipe yellow royal icing

confectioners' (icing) sugar, for dusting

3½oz (100g) white rolled fondant (sugarpaste)

edible glue

EQUIPMENT

baby shoe cookie cutter

3 piping bags (see p.12) with fine (1–2) tips (nozzles)

3 squeezy bottles or piping bags with thick (4) tips

toothpicks (cocktail sticks)

small or medium flower, star, or circle cutters

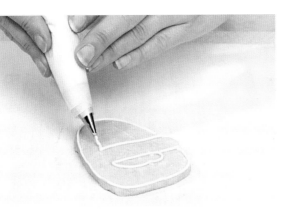

1 Outline and flood the cookies using a fine tip for the outline and a large tip for the flooding, following the steps on pp.18–19.

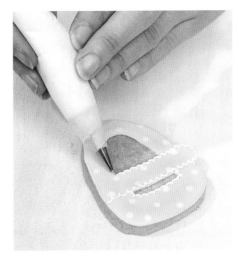

2 Add polka dots while the icing is still wet by dropping dots of white into the icing, following the wet-on-wet technique on p.19.

3 When the icing has dried, pipe a border around the cookies using a fine tip.

4 Dust the countertop (work surface) with confectioners' sugar and roll out the white rolled fondant. Using a cutter, cut out flowers or buttons (see p.23) for the shoe fasteners and attach with edible glue.

bunting

This cookie bunting is perfect for any celebration, from a birthday party to a wedding, and can be made in any color scheme or design. These cookies have been decorated with rolled fondant (sugarpaste), which is quick and simple to use and can be embossed with a design. They also look beautiful decorated with flooded royal icing.

YOU WILL NEED:
12 triangle cookies made
    from a recipe on pp.13–14,
    using the bunting
    template, p.126
confectioners' (icing) sugar,
    for dusting
4oz (125g) blue rolled
    fondant (sugarpaste)
    (see p.20)
4oz (125g) white rolled
    fondant
4oz (125g) pink rolled
    fondant
4oz (125g) yellow rolled
    fondant
edible glue
2.2yd (2m) ribbon

EQUIPMENT
rolling pin
triangle cookie template
knife
skewer
heart, star, and flower
    cutters
embossing tool (optional)

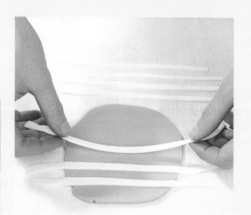

1 Dust the countertop (work surface) with confectioners' sugar and roll out the rolled fondant for the cookies that will have a plain background. Cut out the template on p.126 and use it to cover the cookies following the steps on p.20. Then, while the rolled fondant is still soft, use a skewer to make a hole through it corresponding with the holes in the cookies.

2 To make striped rolled fondant cookies, roll out some colored rolled fondant as normal. Then roll out some white rolled fondant to ⅛in (3mm) thick, cut it into thin strips and lay them over the colored rolled fondant. Make the strips slightly narrower than the stripes you want, as the icing will be rolled and will therefore spread.

3 Gently roll over the strips with a rolling pin so that they become incorporated into the colored rolled fondant as stripes.

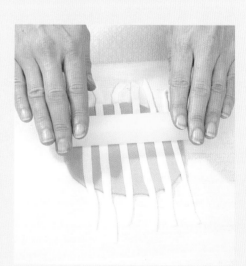

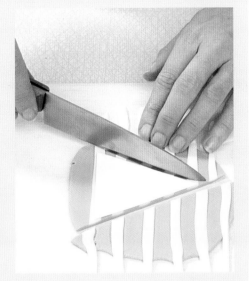

4 Using the bunting template used to make the cookies, cut out the striped rolled fondant.

5 Attach the striped rolled fondant to the cookies in the usual way, following the steps on p.20.

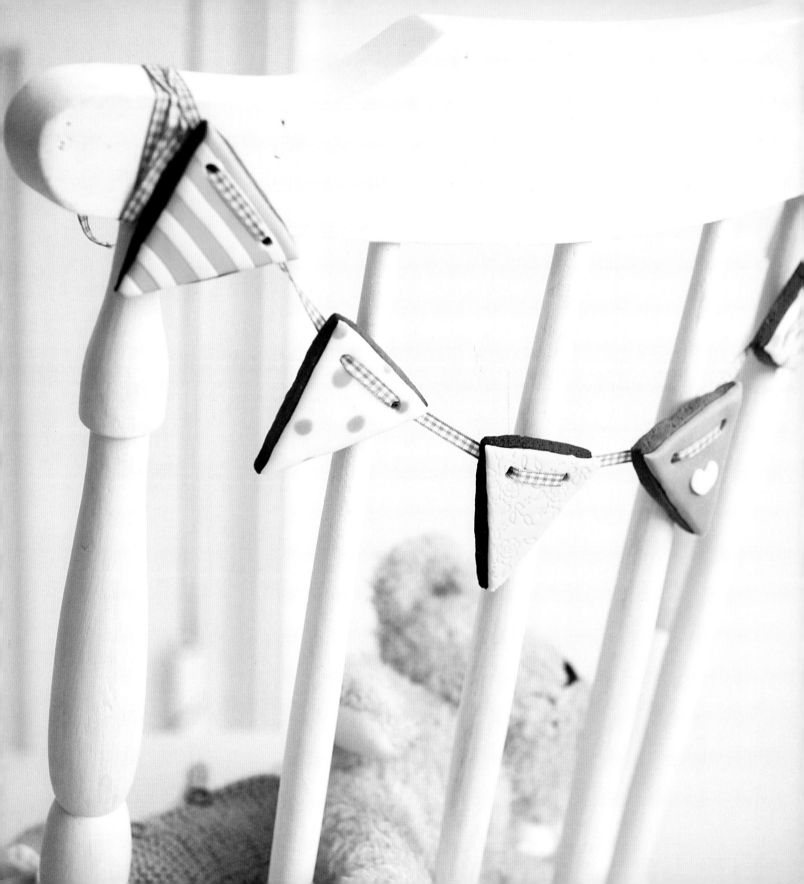

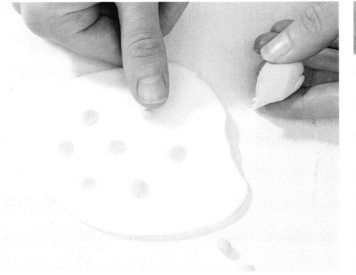 

6 To make polka-dot icing, roll out some white rolled fondant. Then roll some small balls of colored rolled fondant between your fingers and squash these down onto the white rolled fondant using your thumb. When all the balls are in place, gently roll over the rolled fondant to incorporate the dots into it. Cut out the rolled fondant and attach it to the cookies as above.

7 To emboss the icing, lightly push a cutter or embossing tool into the rolled fondant while it is still soft. Cut the rolled fondant out and attach it to the cookies as above.

8 Use cutters to cut out hearts, stars, and flowers, then attach to the iced cookies.

9 When the cookies are dry, loop the ribbon through them to make a chain of bunting.

balloons

These colorful balloon lollipops are perfect for a children's party or as a birthday gift for a big kid. Add extra detail with white polka dots and a ribbon trim, or go for simple pastel colors for a more sophisticated look.

YOU WILL NEED:

12 balloon lollipop cookies
   (see p.15) made from
   a recipe on pp.13–14,
   using a cookie cutter
¼ recipe each pink, yellow,
   blue, green, and white
   royal icing (see pp.16–17)
2.2yd (2m) ribbon

EQUIPMENT

balloon cookie cutter
12 lollipop sticks
4 piping bags (see p.12) with
   fine (1–2) tips (nozzles)
5 squeezy bottles or piping
   bags with thick (4) tips
toothpick (cocktail stick)

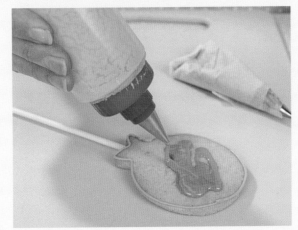

1 Outline and flood the cookies using a fine tip for the outline and a thick tip for the flooding, following the steps on pp.18—19.

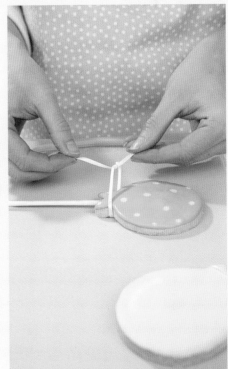

2 While the icing is still wet, add polka dots by dropping dots of wet white icing onto the cookie using the wet-on-wet icing technique on p.19.

3 To ice a reflection line, while the icing is still wet, pipe a curved line of wet white icing toward the top of each cookie.

4 Tie a length of ribbon around the bottom of each balloon.

summer daisies

These beautiful daisy cookies are perfect for a summer party. Using a daisy plunger cutter makes these detailed flowers easy to create. Whilst for other cookies, standard cutters are fine, using a plunger cutter here adds the details on the petals, giving a superior finish. I have used white and pale yellow for these summer daisies, but you could use the same cutter with hot pinks and purples for striking gerberas.

YOU WILL NEED:
12 round cookies made from a recipe on pp.13–14, using a cookie cutter
confectioners' (icing) sugar, for dusting
14oz (400g) white rolled fondant (sugarpaste)
edible glue
14oz (400g) yellow rolled fondant (see p.20)
¼ recipe white or yellow royal icing (see p.16–17)

EQUIPMENT
rolling pin
round cookie cutter
knife
daisy plunger cutters in 3 sizes
toothpick (cocktail stick)
1 piping bag (see p.12) with 1 fine (1—2) tip (nozzle), for piping

2 Attach the daisy to the cookie with sugar glue and curl up the ends of the petals with a toothpick.

1 Dust the countertop (work surface) with confectioners' sugar and roll out the white rolled fondant. Cover the cookies following the steps on p.20. Dust the flower cutters with confectioners' sugar so that the rolled fondant does not stick. Roll the rolled fondant to a thickness of ⅛in (3mm). Cut out a daisy with the largest cutter, then press down the plunger to emboss the petal design.

3 Repeat the process with the middle and small daisy cutters, attaching one above the other in the center of the flower and curling up the ends of all the petals.

4 To make the flower center, roll a small ball of white rolled fondant between your fingers and use your thumb to flatten it into a disk with a slightly raised center.

5 Attach the disk of rolled fondant to the center of the flower and, using a fine tip, pipe dots of royal icing over the disk.

vintage corsages

Inspired by old-fashioned ribbon and 1950s enamelware, these kitsch corsages make a lovely addition to a picnic basket or tea party table. Go for reds and blues for a more traditional look or opt for pastel colors for a summer wedding. You can vary the design as you wish with hearts and stars, different borders, and cute ribbon details (see the Variation, overleaf).

YOU WILL NEED:

12 round cookies made from a recipe on pp.13–14, using a cookie cutter confectioners' (icing) sugar, for dusting

9oz (250g) each red, white, and blue rolled fondant (sugarpaste) (see p.20)

¼ recipe each red, blue, and white royal icing (see pp.16—17)

edible glue

EQUIPMENT

rolling pin
round cookie cutter
knife
toothpick (cocktail stick)
3 piping bags (see p.12) with fine (1–2) tips (nozzles)
2 small round cutters, in 2 different sizes

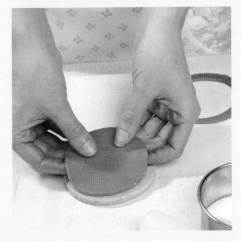

1 Cover a batch of round cookies with red, blue, or white rolled fondant, following the steps on p.20.

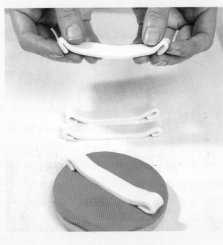

2 Cut 4 strips of icing the width of the cookie and fold over the ends.

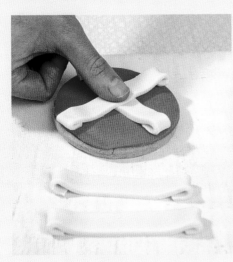

3 Attach the strips to the cookie, squashing them in the center with your thumb as you add each one.

4 Use the toothpick to curl the edges under.

5 Decorate the ribbons by piping stars or hearts on them with a fine tip.

6 Roll a ball of rolled fondant between your fingers and then squash it into a disk. Attach it to the center of the cookie.

7 With a fine tip, pipe a border around the disk and some polka dots around the edge of the cookie. Finish with a ring of tiny polka dots around the disk.

8 Finally, make some buttons using two different-sized cutters (see p.23) and attach them to the center of the corsage.

VARIATION

Alternatively, cut 8 fine strips of rolled fondant in 2 different colors. Cut a "V" in one end to form the ribbon ends, then attach them to the cookie in alternating colors.

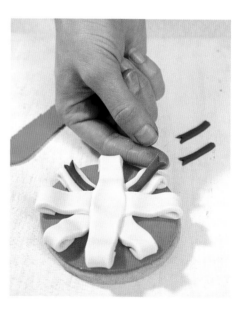

tulips and butterfly

A bunch of tulip cookie lollipops makes a fun, edible alternative to a traditional bunch of flowers. They are perfect for any occasion, from birthdays and Valentines to a cheery "get well soon" gift. Add a butterfly for extra detail, then tie them with a beautiful bow or display them in a decorated flowerpot for a spring event.

YOU WILL NEED:
11 tulip and 1 butterfly cookie lollipops (see p.15) made from a recipe on pp.13–14, using the tulip template on p.125 and a butterfly cookie cutter
½ recipe each yellow and purple royal icing, and ¼ recipe white royal icing (see pp.16–17)

EQUIPMENT
butterfly cookie cutter
12 lollipop sticks
4 piping bags (2 with 1—2 tips and 2 with 4 tips)
toothpick (cocktail stick)

1 Outline and flood the cookies using a fine tip for the outline and a thick tip for the flooding, following the steps on pp.18—19.

2 When the tulips are dry, outline them a second time, with a fine tip.

3 To ice the butterfly, outline and flood the cookies using a fine tip for the outline and a thick tip for the flooding, using two separate colors, following the steps on pp.18—19. While the icing is still wet, add colored dots to the top wings by piping a large dot of white icing, with a second smaller dot of yellow icing in the center, using the wet-on-wet technique on p.19.

4 Wet-on-wet marbling is a really effective way to decorate butterflies. While the icing on the bottom of the wings is still wet, using a fine tip, pipe lines of wet icing on the edges of the wings and gently pull the end of a toothpick through them to make a pattern. To finish, pipe a thick line of yellow icing down the center of the butterfly for the body.

hot-air balloons

These Phileas Fogg-style hot-air balloons, complete with cookie clouds, make a great birthday treat for a young explorer or a bon voyage gift for someone setting off on their travels.

YOU WILL NEED:
6 hot-air balloon cookies
   and 6 cloud cookies
   made from a recipe on
   pp.13–14, using the cloud
   template on p.123 and a
   balloon cookie cutter
¼ recipe pale blue royal
   icing (see pp.16–17)
½ recipe white royal icing
¼ recipe yellow royal icing

EQUIPMENT
hot-air balloon cookie cutter
3 piping bags (see p.12) with
   fine (1–2) tips (nozzles)
3 squeezy bottles or piping
   bags with thick (4) tips
toothpick (cocktail stick)

2 Flood alternate sections of the balloons in white and flood the baskets in pale blue or yellow, using a thick tip and following the steps on p.19. Leave them to dry for half an hour. When the icing has dried, fill in the remaining sections in either yellow or pale blue.

1 Outline each cookie using a fine tip, piping lines down the balloons to separate each color. Also outline the shape of the baskets in blue or yellow, following the steps on p.18.

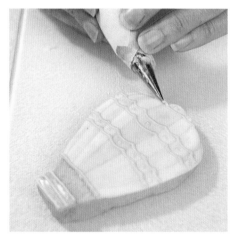

3 Finally, pipe stripes and dots of icing over the balloons for added detail and add some stripes to the baskets.

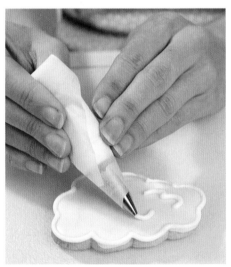

4 Outline and flood the cloud cookies using a fine tip for the outline and a thick tip for the flooding, following the steps on pp.18–19. When they are dry, outline them again and add some lines of white icing in the center to give them texture.

chapter 2

fun for children

All of the colorful projects in this chapter are designed to make with or for children: bake apple cookies to take to school, create colorful sea creatures or fun animal faces, make glittery tiaras with little princesses, or trains and boats for young adventurers.

apples for my teacher

These kitsch apples are perfect for a lunch box or as a gift for a favorite teacher. Make them as a project with children using rolled fondant (sugarpaste) or use royal icing for a more sophisticated finish.

✳ **YOU WILL NEED:**

12 apple cookies made from a recipe on pp.13–14, using a cookie cutter
confectioners' (icing) sugar, for dusting
7oz (200g) each green and red rolled fondant (sugarpaste) (see p.20)
2oz (50g) each dark green and white rolled fondant
1oz (30g) brown rolled fondant
edible glue

EQUIPMENT
rolling pin
apple cookie cutter
knife
leaf plunger cutter
soft paintbrush

1 Dust the countertop (work surface) with confectioners' sugar and roll out the green rolled fondant. Cover the cookies following the steps on p.20, but cut off the stalk part of the rolled fondant.

2 To add the white reflection, roll a thin sausage of white rolled fondant, cut a strip about ⅝in (1.5cm) long, attach it to the cookie, and squash it flat.

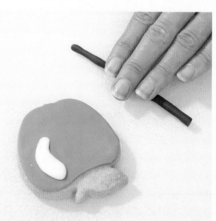

3 To make a stalk, roll a thin sausage of brown rolled fondant and cut it into small pieces for each apple. Attach the stalks to the cookies.

4 Using a leaf plunger cutter, cut out leaves from dark green rolled fondant. Push down the plunger so that the leaves are veined, then release the leaves and attach a leaf to each cookie with edible glue.

animal faces

These cute animal faces are simple to make and do not require any tools other than a round or wavy-edged cookie cutter. They are made by simply modeling rolled fondant (sugarpaste), making them a fun and easy project for children and adults alike. The quantities of rolled fondant are enough to make two cookies in each design.

YOU WILL NEED:
10 round cookies made from a recipe on pp.13–14, using a cookie cutter
confectioners' (icing) sugar, for dusting
3½oz (100g) each brown, pink, white, and black rolled fondant (sugarpaste) (see p.20)
2oz (50g) gray rolled fondant
edible glue

EQUIPMENT
rolling pin
round cookie cutter
wavy-edged cookie cutter
knife

1 For the bear, cover the cookie with rolled fondant following the steps on p.20. To make the ears, roll a ball of brown rolled fondant and a smaller ball (about half the size) of pink rolled fondant. Using your thumb, squash the brown ball into a flat ear shape, leaving a raised edge at the top, which will form the edge of the ear. Squash the pink ball with your thumb and attach it to the brown ball, leaving a thin border at the top for the edge of the ear. Using a knife, cut off the bottom of the ear in a slight curve. Repeat the process to make a second ear and attach the ears to either side of the cookie.

2 For the eyes, roll a small ball of white rolled fondant and a smaller ball of black. Make the white ball oblong and squash it with your thumb. Squash the black ball and attach to the bottom of the white oblong. Repeat for the second eye. For the cheeks, roll 2 balls of white rolled fondant (twice the size of the eyes). Squash them to make circles and mark dots using a toothpick. For the nose, roll a small ball of pink icing. Pinch one end into a "V" shape, flatten slightly, and attach to the cookie.

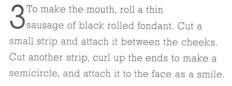

3 To make the mouth, roll a thin sausage of black rolled fondant. Cut a small strip and attach it between the cheeks. Cut another strip, curl up the ends to make a semicircle, and attach it to the face as a smile.

4 To make the cat, cover the cookies with black rolled fondant as above. Make eyes, a nose, and cheeks, following the method in step 2.

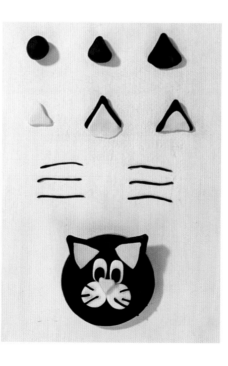

5 To make the ears, roll two balls of black rolled fondant. Pinch the tops of the balls into triangles and flatten the bottoms with your thumb. Cut 2 small triangles of pink rolled fondant and attach these to the inside of the ears. Then cut off the bottom of the ears in a slight curve and attach them to the cookie. To add whiskers, roll thin sausages of black rolled fondant between your fingers, cut them into ¾in (2cm) lengths and attach to the cheeks.

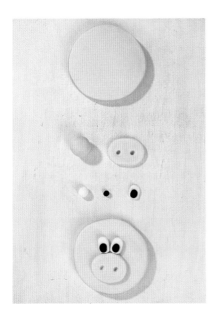

6 To make the pig, dust the countertop (work surface) with confectioners' sugar, then roll out the pink rolled fondant. Cover the cookies following the steps on p.20. Roll a ball of pink rolled fondant, flatten it and make 2 indents for the nose. Attach the nose to the bottom half of the cookie. Make the eyes following the method in step 2 and attach them above the nose.

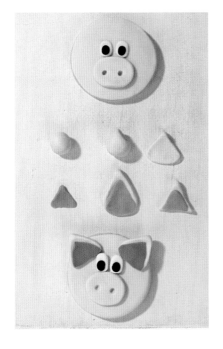

7 Make the ears following the same method for making the ears for the cat in step 5.

8 To make the dog, inlay a patch of gray rolled fondant into white rolled fondant, using the method on p.20. Use this rolled fondant to cover the cookie, following the steps on p.20.

9 To make the eyes, nose, and cheeks, follow the method in step 2. To make the tongue, roll a small ball of pink rolled fondant between your fingers, pinch the top into a teardrop shape, then squash it flat and attach it below the cheeks. To make the ears, roll 2 long teardrop shapes of icing between your fingers, then flatten them. Fold one of the ears over on itself and then attach the ears to the cookie.

10 To make the sheep, cut a circle of white rolled fondant using the wavy side of the cookie cutter if you have one. Roll a ball of black rolled fondant between your fingers. Squeeze the middle of the ball to make it oblong and pinch 2 ears either side at the top. Flatten the ball to shape it into the face of the sheep and attach it to the center of the cookie.

11 Make the eyes following the method in step 2, and attach them to the face. Finally, roll a small ball of pink rolled fondant and then squash it into a disk with your thumb. Attach this to the face as a nose.

princess tiaras and wands

Little princesses will love these sparkly tiaras and wands. They look gorgeously girly, with glitter and ribbons for added detail. Alternatively, make black and orange wands for young wizards using the designs on p. 96.

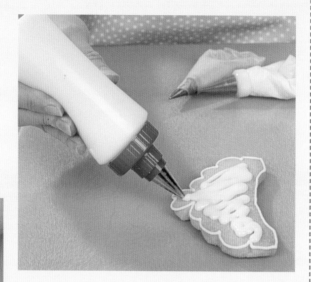

1 For the tiaras: Outline and flood the cookies using a fine tip for the outline and a thick tip for the flooding, following the steps on pp.18—19.

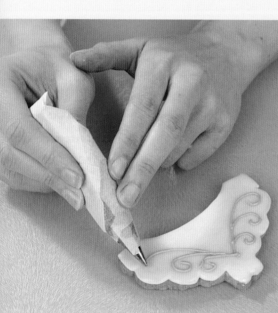

2 When the cookies have dried, fit a piping bag with a fine tip and fill with pink royal icing. Pipe swirls on the cookies.

3 Dust the countertop (work surface) with confectioners' sugar, then roll out some pink rolled fondant. Cut out a heart and some little flowers using the cutters. Attach the heart at the top and the flowers along the bottom of the tiara using edible glue.

YOU WILL NEED:
6 cookies made from a recipe on pp.13—14, using the tiara template on p.124
6 star cookie lollipops (see p.15), made using a cookie cutter
½ recipe white royal icing (see pp.16—17)
½ recipe pink royal icing
confectioners' (icing) sugar, for dusting
3½oz (100g) each pink and white rolled fondant (sugarpaste) (see p.20)
edible glue
edible glitter
little round silver dragees

EQUIPMENT
rolling pin
star cookie cutter
12 lollipop sticks
2 piping bags (see p.12) with fine (1—2) tips (nozzles)
2 squeezy bottles or piping bags with thick (4) tips
toothpicks (cocktail sticks)
medium heart cutter
medium flower cutter
waxed (greaseproof) paper
2.2yd (2m) ribbon

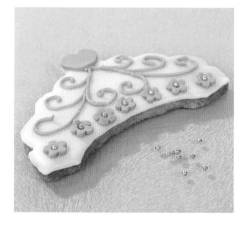

4 Stick little round silver dragees in the center of the flowers for added detail.

5 Put the cookies on some waxed paper and generously sprinkle with glitter, shaking off any excess. Return any excess glitter to its container.

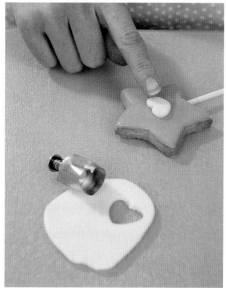

6 For the wands: Outline and flood the star cookies with pink royal icing, using a fine tip for the outline and a thick tip for the flooding, following the steps on pp.18–19. Dust the countertop with confectioners' sugar, then cut out a heart from white rolled fondant using a cutter and attach it to the center of each star.

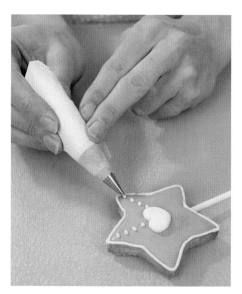

7 Use piping icing to pipe around the edge of the star and also to pipe lines of dots from the center out to each of the points.

8 Finally, sprinkle glitter over each star and tie a ribbon bow to the stick.

ladybugs

These cute ladybugs (ladybirds) are perfect for a garden tea party or for making with children on a wet summer's afternoon. Turn them into love bugs by replacing the black spots on the wings with pink or white hearts.

✳

YOU WILL NEED:
12 cookies made from a
   recipe on pp.13–14, using
   ladybug template on p.124
confectioners' (icing) sugar,
   for dusting
9oz (250g) each of black
   and red, and 2oz (50g)
   white rolled fondant
   (sugarpaste) (see p.20)
edible glue

EQUIPMENT
rolling pin
small heart-shaped cutter
knife
soft paintbrush

1 Dust the countertop (work surface) with confectioners' sugar and roll out the black rolled fondant. Cut out a strip, rounding one end for the head, and attach it down the middle of each cookie. Cut it off at the other end, following the line of the cookie.

2 Cut out a circle of red rolled fondant and cut it in half. Attach each of the halves to the cookie as wings, joining the two halves in the center by the head.

3 Roll 2 small balls of white rolled fondant, 6 small balls of black rolled fondant, and 2 tiny balls of black rolled fondant between your fingers for each cookie. Squash each of the balls into little circles, using your thumb. Stick the tiny black circles to the white circles, and attach these to the head as eyes. Then attach the remaining black circles to the wings as spots.

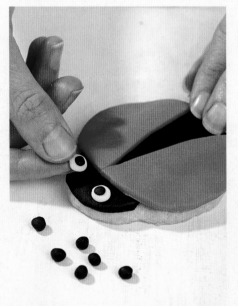

4 Roll a long thin sausage of black rolled fondant, cut into ⅝in (1.5cm) lengths, and attach 2 to each cookie as antennae. Also cut out some hearts from some rolled-out fondant with a small cutter. Stick the hearts on the end of the antennae, bending them so that they stand up a little.

sailing boats

These colorful sailing boats are ideal for a picnic on the beach or for a summer party. Add polka dots and numbers on the sails for children or leave them plain for a gift for a grown-up sailor.

YOU WILL NEED:
12 yacht cookies made from a recipe on pp.13–14, using a cookie cutter
¼ recipe pale blue royal icing (see pp.16–17)
¼ recipe red royal icing
½ recipe white royal icing

EQUIPMENT
yacht cookie cutter
3 piping bags (see p.12) with fine (1–2) tips (nozzles)
3 squeezy bottles or piping bags with thick (4) tips
toothpick (cocktail stick)

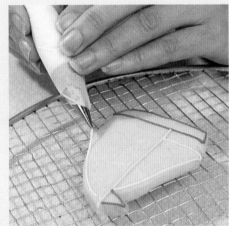

1 Pipe a colored line down the center of the cookie for the mast, then outline the sails, hull, and flag using a thin tip, following the steps on pp.18–19.

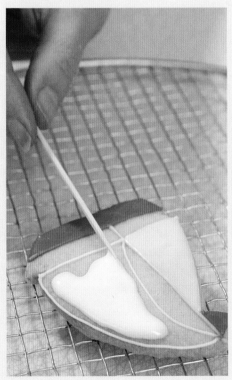

2 Flood the sails in white icing and flood the hull and flag in a different color, following the steps on p.19.

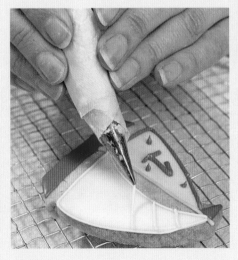

3 Outline the sails again and add dots, stripes, and numbers to decorate them.

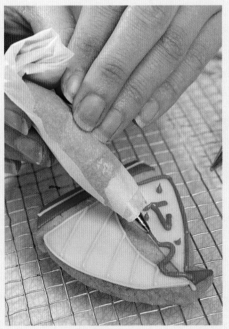

4 Finally, pipe a wiggly line of colored icing down the mast as a rope.

train set

My Dad bought these cookie cutters for me when he was on a train trip. They look great decorated with colorful rolled fondant and button wheels for children, or flooded in dark colors for big kids. So thanks, Dad: these cookies are for you.

YOU WILL NEED:
6 train cookies and
  6 carriage cookies
  made from a recipe on
  pp.13–14, using cookie
  cutters
confectioners' (icing) sugar,
  for dusting
4oz (125g) each pale blue,
  white, and red rolled
  fondant (sugarpaste)
  (see p.20)
edible glue

EQUIPMENT
rolling pin
train and carriage cookie
  cutters
toothpicks (cocktail sticks)
soft paintbrush
3 round cutters
knife

1 Dust the countertop (work surface) with confectioners' sugar, then roll out the blue rolled fondant and use to cover the engine cookies, following the steps on p.20. Repeat with the white rolled fondant for the carriages.

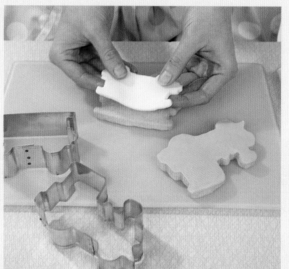

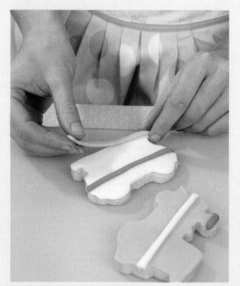

2 Roll out the red, white, or blue rolled fondant to ⅛in (3mm) thick and, using a knife, cut it into strips about ¼in (5mm) wide. Attach the strips along the center of the engine and carriages and along the tops of the funnel and carriages.

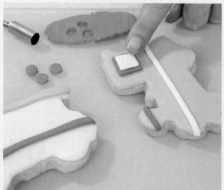

3 To make the windows, either cut squares of rolled fondant using a knife or cutter, or cut small circles of rolled fondant using a cutter. Attach these to the engine and carriages.

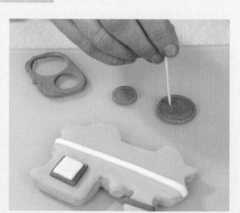

4 Finally, make button wheels by cutting circles of rolled fondant with a cutter. Using a slightly smaller cutter, imprint a smaller circle by pushing the cutter into the icing, but not all the way through. Mark 4 buttonholes in the icing using a toothpick.

under the sea

These sea creatures look great in bright colors, which really stand out on gingerbread cookies. Add spots and stripes for extra detail and finish them with piped fins and eyes.

YOU WILL NEED:

3 each of angel fish, clown fish, octopus, and seahorse cookies made from a recipe on pp.13–14, using the templates on p.126

¼ recipe each white, pink, orange, purple, blue, and brown royal icing (see pp.16–17)

EQUIPMENT

6 piping bags (see p.12) with fine (1–2) tips (nozzles)
5 squeezy bottles or piping bags with thick (4) tips
toothpicks (cocktail sticks)

1 Outline and flood the angel fish with white royal icing, using a fine tip for the outline and a thick tip for the flooding, following the steps on pp.18–19. While the icing is still wet, add pink stripes or spots to the body by piping lines or dots of wet icing into the icing, following the wet-on-wet technique on p.19.

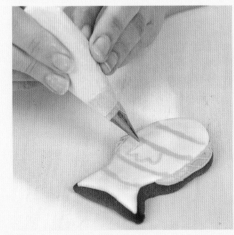

2 In the same way, outline and flood the clown fish, adding orange stripes or spots. Leave the fish to dry, then pipe detailing on the fins and tail using a fine tip.

3 Outline each octopus in purple icing, using a thin tip, piping all of the individual tentacles, then flood the octopus and add polka dots as above. When the octopus has dried, outline it again in a different color. (Using piping icing in the same color as the spots, as here, is very effective.)

4 Outline the seahorses with a fine tip, piping a scalloped edge down the back. Flood and add the polka dots as above. When all the sea creatures have dried, add eyes by piping a dot of brown piping icing.

teddy bears

These cute teddy bears make a lovely gift for a young child or expectant mom. Add colorful dungarees for added detail or leave them plain for a traditional look.

YOU WILL NEED:
12 cookies made from a recipe on pp.13–14, using the teddy bear templates on p.125
confectioners' (icing) sugar, for dusting
9oz (250g) brown rolled fondant (sugarpaste) (see p.20)
2oz (50g) each blue, pink, and white rolled fondant
1oz (30g) dark brown rolled fondant
edible glue

EQUIPMENT
rolling pin
small heart cutter
toothpick (cocktail stick)
small round cutter

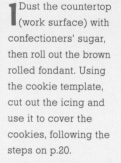

1 Dust the countertop (work surface) with confectioners' sugar, then roll out the brown rolled fondant. Using the cookie template, cut out the icing and use it to cover the cookies, following the steps on p.20.

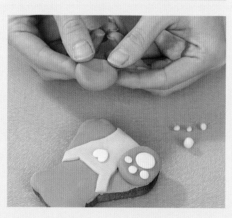

2 Cut out the dungarees from the blue rolled fondant, using the template on p.125; also cut out a small heart from white rolled fondant with the cutter. Attach a pair of dungarees to each bear and add a heart on top.

3 To add the feet, roll 2 balls of brown rolled fondant. Squash the sides of the balls to make them slightly oblong, then flatten them with your thumb. Attach them to the cookie. Then, for each foot, roll one small and 3 tiny balls of pink rolled fondant. Squash them flat and attach them to the feet.

4 To make the face, roll 2 small balls of pink rolled fondant, squash them flat, and attach to the ears. Roll another, slightly bigger, ball of pink rolled fondant. Squash the top to make a triangular shape and flatten it. Using a toothpick, mark a line from the top to two-thirds of the way down the triangle. Then use the edge of a round cutter to indent a semicircle for the smile. To finish each cookie, roll one small ball and 2 tiny balls of dark brown rolled fondant. Attach the tiny balls as eyes and stick the larger ball to the top of the muzzle as a nose.

chapter 3

holiday cookies

Fill your home with the festive smell of home baking with these projects for the whole family to enjoy: bake decorations for your Christmas tree, keep children entertained with Glittery Ghosts for Halloween, and make cute chicks and bunnies for Easter.

scandinavian birds

These lovely bird cookies were inspired by a design in Clare Young's beautiful book on Scandinavian needlecraft. Hang them on ribbons as festive decorations or simply enjoy them by the fire with a hot drink.

YOU WILL NEED:

12 cookies made from
   a recipe on pp.13–14,
   using the bird template
   on p.126
1 recipe white royal icing
   (see pp.16–17)
¼ recipe blue, green, or
   beige royal icing
2.2yd (2m) ribbon

EQUIPMENT

3 piping bags (see p.12) with
   fine (1–2) tips (nozzles)
1 squeezy bottle or piping
   bag with thick (4) tip
toothpick (cocktail stick)

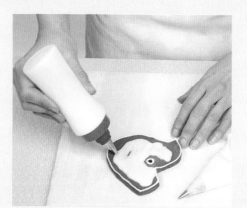

1 Bake a batch of cookies with a hole in the top for the ribbon to pass through. When they are cool, outline and flood them using a fine tip for the outline and a thick tip for the flooding, following the steps on pp.18–19.

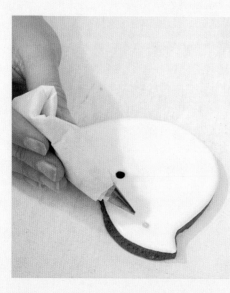

2 Pipe a dot of blue icing in the center of each head for the eye.

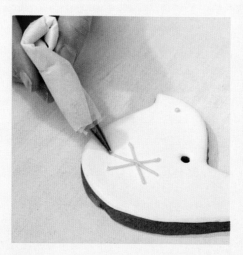

3 Pipe a simple star or leaf design on the body of each bird in blue, green, or beige.

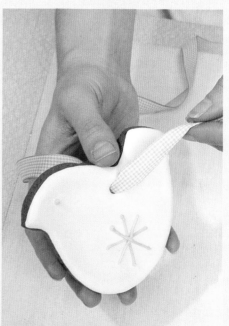

4 Thread a length of ribbon through the hole and hang up as decorations.

baubles

These bauble cookies make lovely Christmas tree decorations. Go for turquoise, red, and white for a vintage look or opt for richer colors, such as purples or reds, for a traditional festive look. Making these cookies from gingerbread makes your house smell wonderfully festive.

YOU WILL NEED:
12 cookies made from a
    recipe on pp.13–14,
    using assorted bauble
    cookie cutters
½ recipe each white,
    turquoise, and red royal
    icing (see pp.16–17)
edible glitter
2.2yd (2m) ribbon

EQUIPMENT
bauble cookie cutters
3 piping bags (see p.12) with
    fine (1–2) tips (nozzles)
    and 2 with thick (4) tips
spatula or table knife
toothpick (cocktail stick)

1 Bake a batch of cookies with a hole in the top. Outline and flood them, using a fine tip for the outline and a thick tip for the flooding, following the steps on pp.18–19.

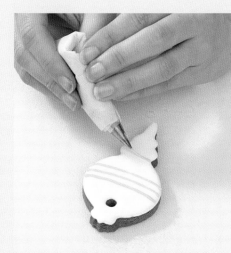

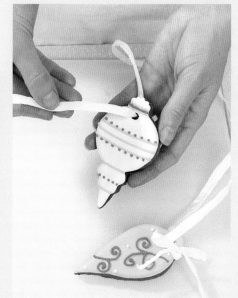

2 With fine tips, pipe simple patterns onto the cookies in different colors.

3 While the cookies are still wet, sprinkle glitter over them. To get a light, even covering, put some glitter on the end of a spatula or table knife and gently tap the side.

4 Finally, thread ribbon through the cookies so that they can be hung up.

polka-dot presents

These colorful presents make a lovely Christmas gift, or change the colors to use them all year round. Once you have learned to make the icing bows, you can use them on all sorts of different cookies. If you don't have time to make fondant bows, simply cover the cookies with rolled fondant and tie them with real ribbons.

YOU WILL NEED:

12 cookies made from a recipe on pp.13—14, using a square cookie cutter

confectioners' (icing) sugar, for dusting

7oz (200g) white rolled fondant (sugarpaste)

7oz (200g) red rolled fondant (see p.20)

edible glue

EQUIPMENT

square cookie cutter
rolling pin
knife
paintbrush or kitchen paper (optional)

1 Dust the countertop (work surface) with confectioners' sugar. Make some polka-dot rolled fondant using the technique on p.20. Cut out squares of rolled fondant the same size as the cookies.

2 Cover the cookies with the polka-dot rolled fondant, following the steps on p.20. Roll out some icing to ⅛in (3mm) thick and cut strips of icing about ⅜in (1cm) wide. Attach 2 strips to each cookie for the ribbons.

3 To make a bow, cut out a strip of red rolled fondant about ⅜in (1cm) wide and twice the length that you would like the bow to be. Take one end and fold it into the center, making sure that the curl stands open (you can use the end of a paintbrush or some rolled-up kitchen paper to support it). Fold in the other half so that the ends meet in the center. Lay the bow on another, slightly thinner, strip of rolled fondant. Fold in the ends of this strip and turn the bow over. Finally, gently squeeze the sides to shape the bow.

4 To make the ribbon tails for each cookie, cut a strip of rolled fondant ⅜in (1cm) wide. Cut it in half and cut little triangles in the ends. Attach the strips to the center of the cookie and stick the bow on top.

christmas puddings

These colorful cookies were inspired by a vintage Christmas card that my mom found and are a kitsch take on the traditional English Christmas pudding. Make them with gingerbread dough for some Chrismas spice.

1 Dust the countertop (work surface) with confectioners' sugar and roll out the red, blue, and green rolled fondant. Roll small balls of white rolled fondant and squash them onto the 3 different-colored rolled fondants with your thumb. Gently roll over the rolled fondant with a rolling pin to incorporate the polka dots, as described on p.20.

2 Cut out the rolled fondant and attach it to the cookie following the steps on p.20. Cut out a circle of white rolled fondant. With a knife, cut a wiggly line through the circle.

3 Take half of the circle and attach it to a Christmas pudding. Add a bow made following the steps on p.80.

4 To decorate the top of the pudding, make buttons (see p.23) or use a plunger cutter to cut out holly leaves. Press down the plunger to vein the leaves. To make a simple rose, roll a thin sausage of rolled fondant and squash it with your thumb. Alternatively, cut a strip of rolled fondant and roll it up from one end.

jolly penguins

These fun penguins are great to make with children during the Christmas holidays. Trace the two penguin templates on p.124 and cut them into the different elements to use as cutting guides. Alternatively, if you feel confident, cut out the shapes freehand. Rolled fondant (sugarpaste) can easily be molded into shape, so don't worry about being too accurate.

YOU WILL NEED:
12 cookies made from a
  recipe on pp.13–14, using
  the penguin template
  on p.124
confectioners' (icing) sugar,
  for dusting
3½oz (100g) orange rolled
  fondant (sugarpaste)
  (see p.20)
edible glue
9oz (250g) black rolled
  fondant
3½oz (100g) white rolled
  fondant
3½oz (100g) red rolled
  fondant

EQUIPMENT
rolling pin
knife
toothpick (cocktail stick)

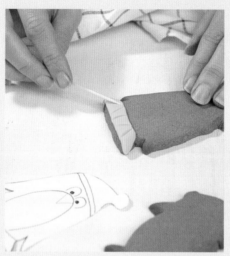

2 Attach the orange rolled fondant to the cookies using edible glue, and mark indents on the feet with a toothpick.

1 Dust the countertop (work surface) with confectioners' sugar and roll out the orange rolled fondant. Cut out the feet using the template as a guide.

3 Roll out some black rolled fondant and, using the template as a guide, cut out the body. Attach it to the cookie and gently roll over it to make it fit.

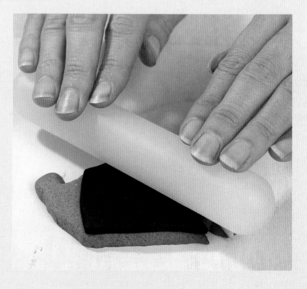

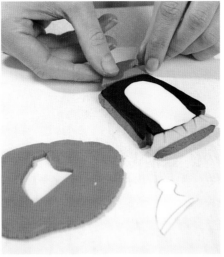

4 Roll out the white rolled fondant and cut out an oval shape for the penguin's tummy. Attach it to each cookie.

5 Roll out the red rolled fondant and cut out the shape of the hat. Attach to the cookie.

6 To make the eyes, roll 2 small balls of white rolled fondant between your fingers. Squash the middle of the balls to make oval shapes and then squash them flat. Attach them to the cookie and stick 2 tiny balls of black rolled fondant to them for the pupils.

7 To make the beak, roll a ball of orange rolled fondant between your fingers. Pinch one end of the ball to make it into a triangle shape, then squash it flat. Attach it to the cookie.

8 To finish the hat, roll a ball of white rolled fondant between your fingers and attach it to the top of the hat as a bobble. Then, finally, roll a thin sausage of white rolled fondant for the trim of the hat. Attach it to the cookie and mark lines along the trim of the hat with a toothpick to give it some texture.

christmas trees

These flooded cookies give a vintage twist to the traditional tree, with soft colors, hearts, dots, and buttons, plus trailing tinsel. They look lovely made with a gingerbread base and ivory flooded icing.

❄ **YOU WILL NEED:**

12 Christmas tree cookies made from a recipe on pp.13–14, using a cookie cutter

1 recipe ivory royal icing (see pp.16–17)

½ recipe each green, red, and turquoise royal icing

1oz (30g) each green, red, and turquoise rolled fondant (sugarpaste) (see p.20)

white edible glitter

EQUIPMENT

4 piping bags (see p.12) with fine (1–2) tips (nozzles) and 1 with thick (4) tip

toothpick (cocktail stick)

paintbrush

various small cutters

2 Pipe on the tinsel, then the polka dots, hearts, or flowers. For the polka dots, keep the tip close to the surface, stop squeezing and then lift off. For a heart, pipe a "V," squeezing harder at the start and end of the "V." For the flowers, pipe small rings of polka dots. To correct any errors in your icing, use a damp paintbrush.

1 Outline and flood the cookies, using a fine tip for the outline and a thick tip for the flooding, following the steps on pp.18–19. Alternatively, cover the cookies with rolled fondant following the steps on p.20.

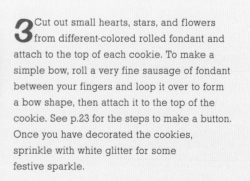

3 Cut out small hearts, stars, and flowers from different-colored rolled fondant and attach to the top of each cookie. To make a simple bow, roll a very fine sausage of fondant between your fingers and loop it over to form a bow shape, then attach it to the top of the cookie. See p.23 for the steps to make a button. Once you have decorated the cookies, sprinkle with white glitter for some festive sparkle.

spring chicks and eggs

These cute chicks and eggs are perfect for a spring table or for prizes for an Easter egg hunt. They look lovely in pastel colors with polka dots and pretty piping for added detail.

YOU WILL NEED:

12 cookies made from a recipe on pp.13–14, using chick and egg cookie cutters

½ recipe pale blue and ¼ recipe white royal icing (see pp.16–17)

confectioners' (icing) sugar

3½oz (100g) pale yellow rolled fondant (sugarpaste) (see p.20)

½ recipe each blue and pale yellow royal icing (see pp.16–17) and ¼ recipe each white and orange

EQUIPMENT

egg and chick cookie cutters

4 piping bags (see p.12) with fine (1–2) tips and 3 with thick (4) tips

toothpick (cocktail stick)

knife

1 Outline and flood the egg cookies, using a fine tip for the outline and a thick tip for the flooding, following the steps on pp.18—19. While the icing is still wet, add polka dots of white icing, using the wet-on-wet technique on p.19.

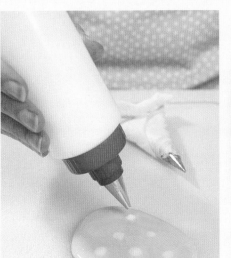

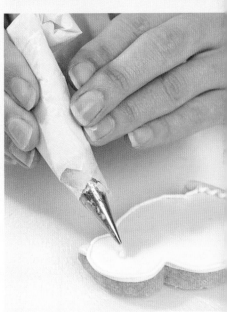

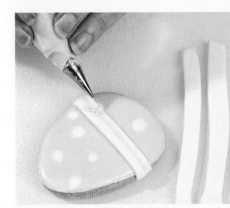

2 When the eggs have dried, dust the countertop (work surface) with confectioners' sugar, cut out strips of pale yellow rolled fondant and lay them over the eggs. Then pipe a design on the yellow strip with pale blue icing, and ice a bow.

3 Outline and flood the chick cookies, using a fine tip for the outline and a thick tip for the flooding, following the steps on pp.18—19. Use pale yellow icing for the body and pale orange icing for the feet and beak. When the icing has dried, pipe an outline of the body of the chick in pale yellow.

4 Pipe a pale blue dot on the head for the eye.

easter bunnies

These bunny cookies are perfect for a spring event or as an alternative to an Easter egg. They look really cute tied with gingham ribbon and decorated in white, pink, and blue. Make half facing forward and half backward so that you have a mixture of cute faces and fluffy tails.

YOU WILL NEED:
12 bunny cookies made from a recipe on pp.13–14, using a cookie cutter
1 recipe white royal icing (see p.16–17)
¼ recipe each pink, brown, and pale blue royal icing
2.2yd (2m) gingham ribbon

EQUIPMENT
2 bunny cookie cutters
4 piping bags (see p.12) with fine (1–2) tips (nozzles)
2 squeezy bottles or piping bags with thick (4) tips
toothpick (cocktail stick)
soft paintbrush

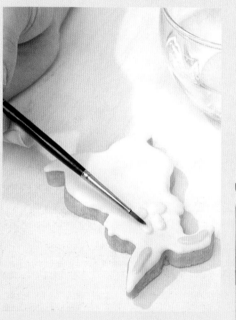

2 Pipe 2 white rounds for cheeks, and 2 white ovals above them for eyes. Smooth them with the paintbrush to soften the outlines a little.

1 Outline and flood the bunnies with white icing, using a fine tip for the outline and a thick tip for the flooding, following the steps on pp.18–19. While the icing is still wet, pipe a stripe of pink icing on each ear, following the wet-on-wet technique on p.19.

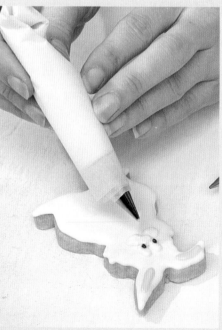

3 Pipe a dot of brown icing toward the bottom of each eye and then pipe a pink dot between the eyes and cheeks for the nose.

4 Using a fine tip, pipe 3 lines of pink icing on each cheek for whiskers.

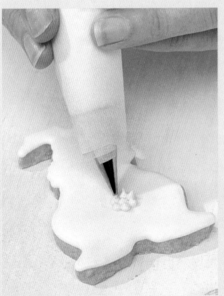

5 To pipe the tail, pipe lots of polka dots close together in a round for a fluffy look.

glittery ghosts

These ghost lollies are ideal for a Halloween party. Make them in ghostly white and green and add lots of glitter for some spooky sparkle.

YOU WILL NEED:

12 ghost cookie lollipops (see p.15) made from a recipe on pp.13–14, using a cookie cutter

½ recipe each white and green, plus ¼ recipe brown royal icing (see pp.16–17)

edible glitter

EQUIPMENT

ghost cookie cutter

12 lollipop sticks

toothpick (cocktail stick)

waxed (greaseproof) paper

3 piping bags (see p.12) with fine (1–2) tips and 2 with thick (4) tips

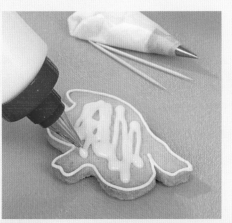

1 Outline and flood the cookies, using a fine tip for the outline and a thick tip for the flooding, following the steps on pp.18–19.

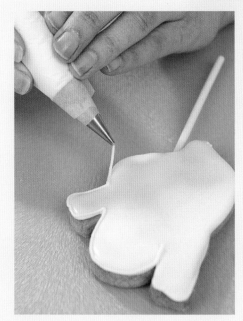

2 Leave the icing to dry for half an hour, then outline the cookies a second time.

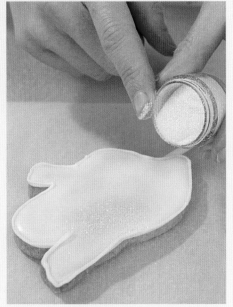

3 Put the cookies on some waxed paper and sprinkle with glitter. Tip the cookies over to pour off any excess glitter. By putting the cookies on waxed paper, you can collect any excess glitter and return it to its container.

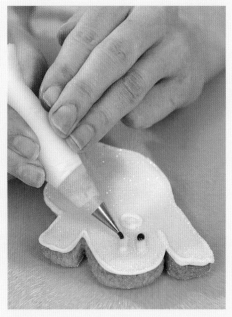

4 Finally, using white icing, pipe a circle for the mouth and 2 ovals for the eyes. Add a dot of brown icing to each eye to finish the cookie.

witches and wizards

These lovely hats are fun to make with children for Halloween treats or as snacks for budding magicians. They work really well on gingerbread cookies.

1 Dust the countertop (work surface) with confectioners' sugar, then roll out the black rolled fondant. Using the templates, cut out 6 witch's hats and 6 wizard's hats and attach them to the cookies, following the steps on p.20.

YOU WILL NEED:
12 cookies made from a recipe on pp.13–14, using the witch's and wizard's hat templates on p.125
confectioners' (icing) sugar, for dusting
9oz (250g) black and 2oz (50g) purple rolled fondant (sugarpaste) (see p.20)
¼ recipe each orange and purple royal icing (see pp.16–17)

EQUIPMENT
rolling pin
knife
2 piping bags (see p.12) with fine (1–2) tips (nozzles)
soft paintbrush

2 Roll out some purple rolled fondant to ⅛in (3mm) thick. Cut some thin strips and attach them around the bottom of each witch's hat as a trim.

3 Using orange piping icing, pipe spiders and webs on the witch's hats. To pipe a web, pipe diagonal lines for structure, then pipe between them with curved lines. To pipe a spider, pipe 4 short lines close together, then add a dot of icing for the body.

4 For the wizard's hats, pipe orange stars and purple dots. To pipe a star, pipe the outline of a five-pointed star and then smooth it over with a damp paintbrush.

chapter 4

love and weddings

Cookies are perfect to celebrate an engagement, or for a wedding reception. Decorate a table with beautiful Broderie Anglaise cookies or kitsch Flower Corsages, or send your wedding guests home with cookie favors, such as Bridal Henna or Contemporary Flowers.

a girl's best friend

These sparkly diamond rings are perfect for an engagement party. Mix them with the polka-dot present cookies on p.80 for a colorful display of rings and gift boxes. You can use dipping alcohol for the silver paint if you have it; otherwise a clear alcohol such as vodka is fine. The silver paint takes a while to dry so leave them at least overnight if possible.

YOU WILL NEED:
12 diamond cookies made
   from a recipe on pp.13–14,
   using a cookie cutter
½ recipe each white and gray
   royal icing (see p.16–17)
white edible glitter
edible silver dusting powder
clear alcohol

EQUIPMENT
diamond ring cookie cutter
3 piping bags (see p.12) with
   fine (1–2) tips (nozzles)
3 squeezy bottles or piping
   bags with thick (4) tips
toothpick (cocktail stick)
waxed (greaseproof) paper
soft paintbrush

1 Outline and flood the diamond at the top of each ring with white icing following the steps on pp.18–19. Allow the icing to dry for a few minutes and then outline the diamond and pipe lines across the middle in the shape of a cut stone.

2 While the icing is still damp, put the cookies on some waxed paper and sprinkle each diamond with white edible glitter. Shake any excess onto the paper and put it back in the container.

3 Outline and flood the cookies with pale gray icing, using a fine tip for the outline and a thick tip for the flooding, following the steps on pp.18–19. Leave to dry completely.

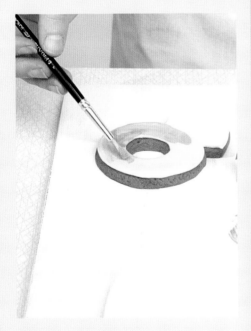

4 Mix some edible silver dusting powder with a little alcohol to make silver paint, then paint the ring part of each cookie with the soft paintbrush.

bridal henna

These cookies are inspired by the beautiful henna designs that some brides have painted on their hands as a symbol of good luck. They are perfect for a summer wedding and look gorgeous in striking colors such as pink or gold.

YOU WILL NEED:
12 round cookies made from a recipe on pp.13–14, using a cookie cutter confectioners' (icing) sugar, for dusting
9oz (250g) white rolled fondant (sugarpaste)
edible glue
¼ recipe pink royal icing (see pp.16–17)

EQUIPMENT
rolling pin
round cookie cutter
tracing paper
dressmaking pins
1 fine tip piping bag (p.12)

1 Cover your cookie with white rolled fondant following the steps on p.20 or outline and flood the cookies, using a fine tip for the outline and a thick tip for the flooding, following the steps on pp.18–19. If you would like to trace the designs onto your cookies (see step 3 below) it is preferable to use rolled fondant as it is easier to mark the design into it.

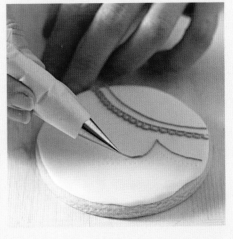

2 Trace the templates for the different henna patterns on p.122 onto some tracing paper. Once you have traced the designs, go over each of them with a pin, pricking the paper at very regular intervals to give lines of dots. It is better to put the holes into the paper before putting it onto the cookie, as the pressure needed to pierce the paper will leave unwanted dents on the cookie. Place the traced design on the cookie and, using a clean pin, mark the design on the cookie by going back over the holes you have already made.

3 Once the design is pricked through, lift off the paper to reveal an imprint of the design on the cookie.

4 Using the fine tip, pipe the design onto the cookie, following the imprinted pattern.

broderie anglaise

These clean and simple-looking cookies are inspired by beautiful, summery broderie anglaise. They are perfect for a wedding, a tea party, or a christening. Make them using a dark cookie, such as gingerbread, so that the cut-out design stands out.

YOU WILL NEED:
12 round cookies made from a recipe on pp.13–14, confectioners' (icing) sugar, for dusting
9oz (250g) white rolled fondant (sugarpaste)
edible glue
¼ recipe white royal icing (see p.16–17)

EQUIPMENT
rolling pin
scalloped-edge round cutter
plastic drinking straws
toothpick (cocktail stick)
dressmaking pins
1 piping bag (see p.12) with fine (1–2) tip (nozzle)

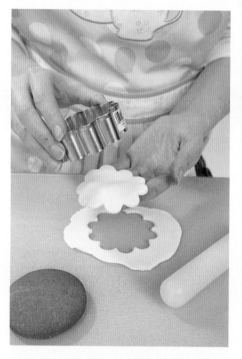

1 Dust the countertop (work surface) with confectioners' sugar, then roll out the white rolled fondant. Cut out flower shapes using the scalloped-edge cutter and attach to the cookies following the steps on p.20.

2 Trace the templates for the different broderie anglaise designs on p.123 onto some tracing paper. Once you have traced the designs, go over each of them with a pin, pricking the paper at very regular intervals to give lines of dots. It is better to put the holes into the paper before putting it onto the cookie, as the pressure needed to pierce the paper will leave unwanted dents on the cookie. Place the traced design on the cookie and, using a clean pin, mark the design on the cookie by going back over the holes you have already made.

3 To make petal shapes with a drinking straw, squash one side of the straw.

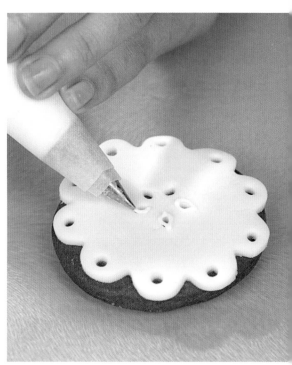

4 To cut out the pattern, push the end of a straw into the rolled fondant, wiggle it slightly to loosen it, then lift off. If necessary, tidy the edges of the holes with a toothpick.

5 Now make the round holes around the edge of the design. If the icing doesn't come out when you lift up the straw, pick out the icing with a toothpick or gently lift up the rolled fondant and release it from underneath.

6 Using the fine tip, pipe around the holes with the white royal icing. Use the tip of a damp paintbrush to tidy the icing, if necessary.

7 Using the same icing, pipe a design on the cookie such as the polka-dot patterns shown.

8 Finally, outline the frilly edge of the cookie with more white icing.

TIP

You can buy eyelet cutters from cook and craft stores to make the cut-out design, or you can use plastic drinking straws to make round or petal-shaped holes in the rolled fondant, as I have done here.

fancy hats

These pretty hats make a perfect gift for Mother's Day or as part of a picnic hamper for a summer event. Decorate them in pastels with polka dots, streamers, and flowers, or go for stylish fondant feathers and simple bows for a sleeker look.

2 Dust the countertop (work surface) with confectioners' sugar and roll out the pink, purple, and white rolled fondants. Then, using the large round cutter, cut out 3 circles from each color slightly larger than the big cookie. Lay each circle of rolled fondant over a hat and smooth it down with your fingers.

1 Stick the small cookies in the center or to one side of the large cookies with royal icing. Alternatively, you could use marshmallows instead of the small cookies.

3 For hats and ribbons with a polka-dot design, use the technique on p.20, again making 3 hats.

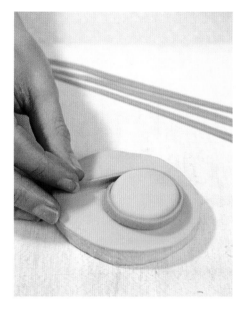

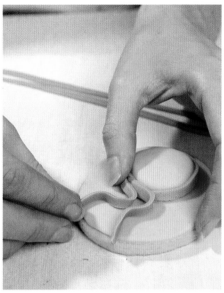

4 Using some of the rolled fondant trimmings, cut out a thin strip and attach it around the middle of the hat.

5 Cut out further strips in various colors and lay them along the hat as streamers.

6 Using a cutter, cut out some flowers and attach them to the hat. Use them to cover any joins in the ribbons.

7 To make a feather, roll a ball of rolled fondant between your fingers. Shape the ball into a long teardrop shape and then squash it flat with your thumb. Use a knife to make small cuts along the edge of the feather.

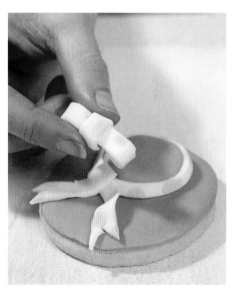

8 See p.80 for the steps to make a matching bow, and attach to the trimming.

contemporary flowers

These beautiful dandelion cookies are ideal for a wedding or summer event. The simple flower design works well in any color scheme. Here, sage green and white give the cookies a lovely fresh look.

YOU WILL NEED:
12 round cookies made from
   a recipe on pp.13–14,
   using a cookie cutter
confectioners' (icing) sugar,
   for dusting
9oz (250g) pale green
   rolled fondant
   (sugarpaste) (see p.20)
edible glue
½ recipe white royal icing
   (see p.16–17)

EQUIPMENT
round cookie cutter
tracing paper
dressmaking pins
1 piping bag (see p.12) with
   1 fine (1–2) tip

1 Dust the countertop (work surface) with confectioners' sugar and roll out the pale green rolled fondant. Cover the cookies following the steps on p.20. Alternatively, outline and flood the cookies, using a fine tip for the outline and a thick tip for the flooding, following the steps on pp.18–19.

2 Trace the templates for the different flower designs on p.122 onto some tracing paper. Once you have traced the designs, go over each of them with a pin, pricking the paper at very regular intervals to give lines of dots. It is better to put the holes into the paper before putting it onto the cookie as the pressure needed to pierce the paper will leave unwanted dents on the cookie.

TIP

If you would like to trace the design onto your cookie (see step 3), it is preferable to use rolled fondant, as it is easier to mark the design into it.

3 Place the traced design on a cookie, and, using a clean pin, mark the design on the cookie by going back over the holes that you have already made. When you lift off the paper, an imprint of the design should be left on the cookie. Repeat on the other cookies.

4 Using the fine tip, pipe the design onto the cookies following the imprinted pattern.

french hearts

These lovely heart cookies are perfect for Valentine's Day, a hen party, or as wedding favors. Dusky pink and brown give them a classic look, but they work very well in any color scheme and so can easily be adapted for an event. The lettering can be piped onto the cookie or can be cut out using a cutter (see suppliers, p.128).

YOU WILL NEED:

12 heart cookies made from a recipe on pp.13–14, using a cookie cutter

1 recipe pink royal icing (see pp.16–17)

confectioners' (icing) sugar, for dusting

3½oz (100g) white flower paste

½ recipe brown royal icing

edible glue

EQUIPMENT

heart cookie cutter

2 piping bags (see p.12) with fine (1–2) tips (nozzles)

1 squeezy bottle or piping bag with thick (4) tip

toothpick (cocktail stick)

letter cutter

soft paintbrush

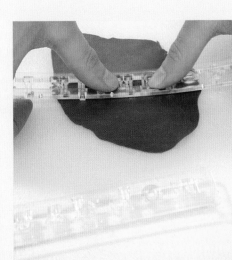

1 Outline and flood the cookies with pink icing, using a fine tip for the outline and a thick tip for the flooding, following the steps on pp.18–19. Color the flower paste dark brown following the steps for coloring rolled fondant on p.20. Dust the countertop (work surface) with confectioners' sugar and roll out the flower paste very thinly (⅛in/1–2mm thick). Firmly press the cutter into the paste to cut out the first letter.

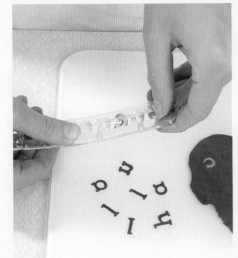

2 Flick or tap the cutter against the edge of the table to release the letter. Repeat with the remaining letters.

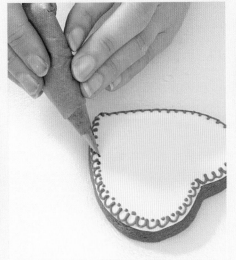

3 With the fine tip, pipe a border around the edge of each cookie.

4 Carefully put the letters in place. Alternatively, pipe the letters onto the cookies with brown piping icing.

blossom and butterflies

These cookies are inspired by the beautiful blossom designs on Japanese porcelain. Use soft pinks and blues for a classic look, or go for bright pink blossom against a white background for something more contemporary. To make very fine flowers and butterflies, as shown here, use flower paste, as this can be rolled very thinly (⅛in/1–2mm). If you do not have flower paste, rolled fondant (sugarpaste) will also work, though the cut-outs will just be slightly thicker.

YOU WILL NEED:
12 round cookies made from a recipe on pp.13–14, using a cookie cutter
confectioners' (icing) sugar, for dusting
9oz (250g) blue rolled fondant (sugarpaste) (see p.20)
¼ recipe brown royal icing (see pp.16–17)
3½oz (100g) pink flower paste
2oz (50g) white flower paste
edible glue

EQUIPMENT
round cookie cutter
knife
pencil
tracing paper
dressmaking pins
1 piping bag (see p.12) with 1 fine (1–2) tip (nozzle)
flower plunger cutter
ball tool (optional)
butterfly plunger cutter
sheet of cardstock (cardboard)
soft paintbrush

1 Dust the countertop (work surface) with confectioners' sugar and roll out the blue rolled fondant. Cover the cookies following the steps on p.20. Trace the template for the branch design on p.124 onto some tracing paper, then go over each with a pin, pricking the paper at very regular intervals to give lines of dots.

2 Remove the paper to reveal the design imprinted on the rolled fondant.

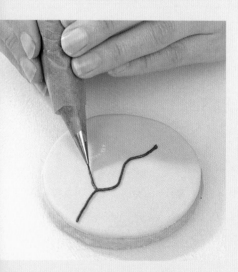

3 Using the fine tip, pipe the branch design onto the cookie following the imprinted pattern.

4 Use the flower plunger cutter to make the blossom.

5 To make the flowers curl up, gently press the centers using a ball tool or the back of a paintbrush. Attach the flowers to the cookie along the branches with edible glue.

6 Cut out the butterflies using the butterfly cutter. To make the wings stand up, concertina a sheet of cardstock and leave the butterflies to dry on it in a "V" shape.

7 When they are dry, attach them to the cookies with edible glue.

flower corsages

These colorful cookies were inspired by the lovely material corsages that you see in stores. Polka dots, stripes, and checked icing all work really well and give the cookies a wonderful vintage feel. Finish them with rolled fondant (sugarpaste) buttons for added detailing and display them on old-fashioned china or simple white plates.

YOU WILL NEED:
12 round cookies made from
    a recipe on pp.13–14,
    using a cookie cutter
confectioners' (icing) sugar
10oz (300g) white rolled
    fondant (sugarpaste)
7oz (200g) each pink, blue,
    and yellow rolled fondant
    (see p.20)
edible glue
¼ recipe white royal icing
    (see pp.16–17)

EQUIPMENT
rolling pin
round cookie cutter
knife
2 sizes flower cutters
toothpick (cocktail stick)
2 sizes round cutters

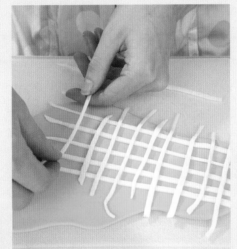

2 Make colorful polka-dot or striped icing, following the steps on p.20. To make checked icing, roll out some pink rolled fondant to ⅛in (3mm) thick. Then roll out some white rolled fondant slightly thinner and cut it into thin strips. Lay the white strips over the pink in both directions so that they form a crisscross pattern.

3 Gently roll over the strips, pressing them into the pink rolled fondant to create a checked pattern.

1 Dust the countertop (work surface) with confectioners' sugar, then roll out the white rolled fondant. Cover the cookies following the steps on p.20.

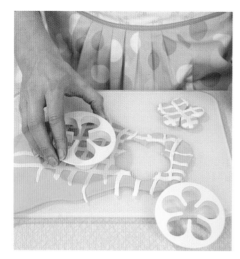

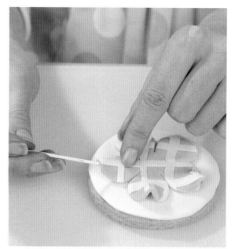

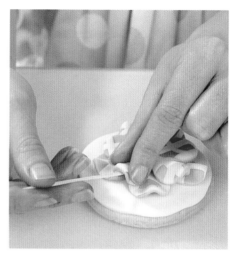

4 Using large and medium 5-petal flower cutters, cut out 2 flower shapes from the rolled fondant.

5 Attach the larger flowers to the cookies. Using a toothpick, lift up the center of each petal at the end and curl the edges of the petals under so that they stand out.

6 Repeat the steps for the medium flower and attach it to the cookie.

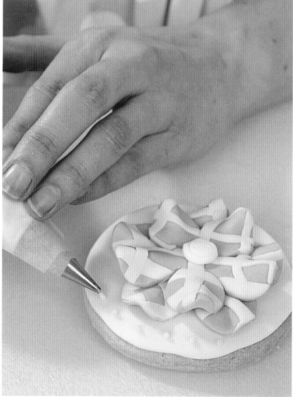

7 Finally, make rolled fondant buttons following the steps on p.23 and add a button to each corsage.

8 Finish by piping a polka dot border of white icing around the edge of the cookies.

templates

Most of the projects in this book use readily available cookie cutters (see suppliers, p.128). Alternatively, you can draw your own template. The templates on the following pages are my own (they can also be downloaded from www.chloecoker.com).

The templates are the correct size so simply trace them onto cardstock (cardboard) or acetate and cut around them, as described in detail on p.10. The templates on pp.122-3 are icing templates so that you can easily replicate the designs. See p.22 for how to transfer these designs onto your cookies.

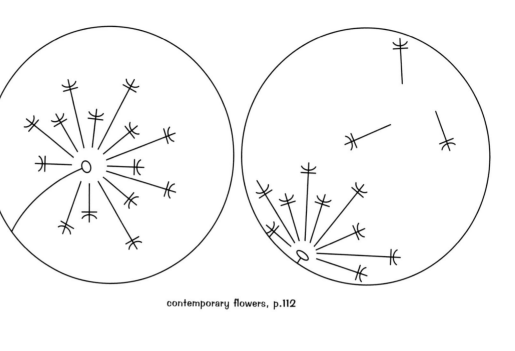

contemporary flowers, p.112

bridal henna, p.102

broderie anglaise, p.104

hot-air balloons, p.48

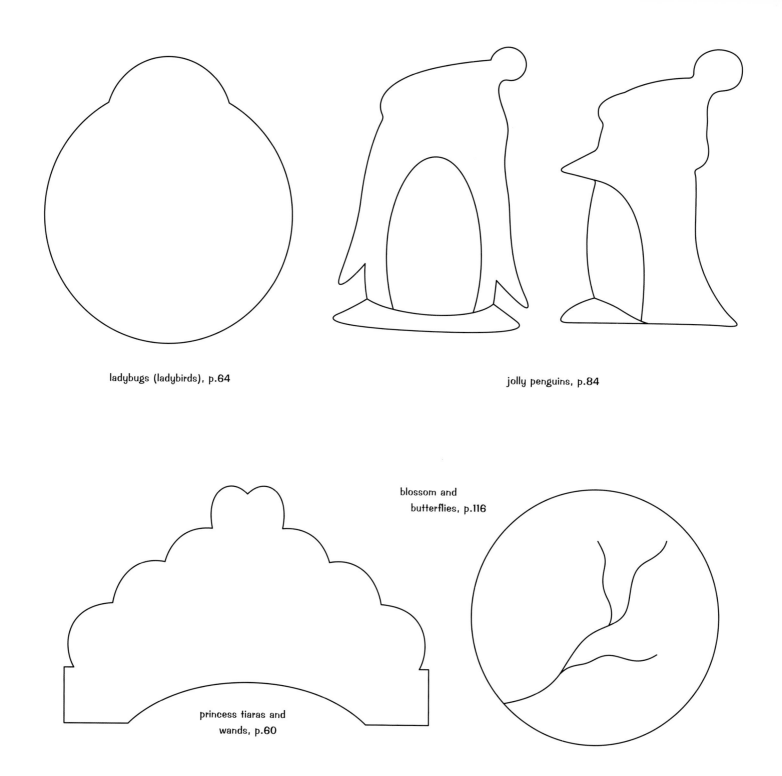

ladybugs (ladybirds), p.64

jolly penguins, p.84

blossom and
butterflies, p.116

princess tiaras and
wands, p.60

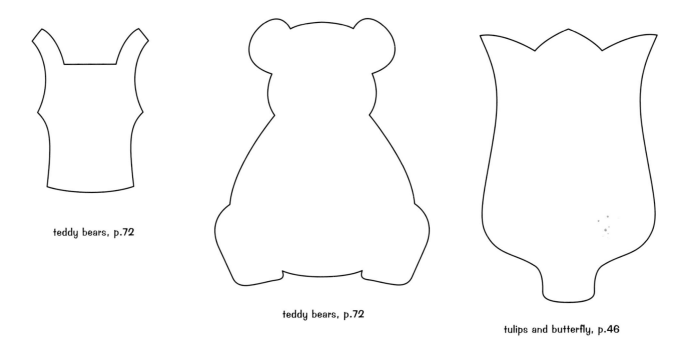

teddy bears, p.72

teddy bears, p.72

tulips and butterfly, p.46

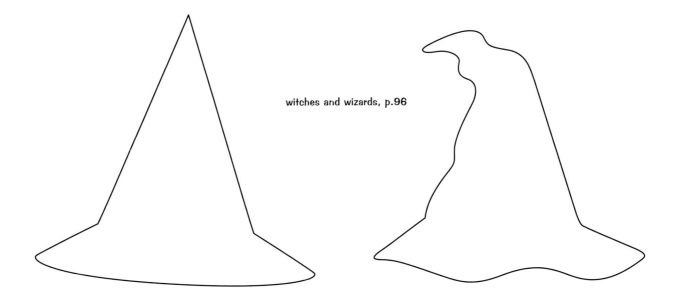

witches and wizards, p.96

under the sea, p.70

scandinavian birds, p.76

bunting, p.34

index

suppliers

IN THE US

Cake Art
www.cakeart.com
For lollipop sticks, covers,
candy melts, brushes, edible
dusting powder, cutters, and
sprinkles.

Fancyflours
www.fancyflours.com
Large online retailer of cake and
candy-making supplies, including
edible diamonds, edible glitter,
unusual cookie cutters including
the pocket watch cutter, and
candy molds.

Michaels
www.michaels.com
Great for lollipop sticks, candy
bags, ribbons, candy molds, cake
decorating tools, craft punches,
and cutters.

N.Y. Cake
www.nycake.com
Baking, cookie, and candy-making
supplies, including cutters,
sprinkles, and edible gold dust.

Sugarcraft
http://sugarcraft.com
Cake, candy, cookie, pie, and
baking products.

Wilton
www.wilton.com
For candy melts, lollipop sticks
and covers, and sprinkles.

IN THE UK

Cakes, Cookies & Crafts
www.cakescookiesandcraftsshop.
co.uk
Tel: 01524 389684
For a great range of cutters
and decorating equipment

Craftcompany
www.craftcompany.co.uk
Tel: 01926 888507
Great range of sugarcraft supplies
with quick and reliable delivery

Ebay
www.ebay.co.uk
Great source of unusual cookie
cutters

John Lewis
www.johnlewis.com
For ribbons and bakeware

Lakeland
www.lakeland.co.uk
Great for baking equipment,
stackable cooling racks, and
disposable piping bags

Squires Kitchen
www.squires-shop.com
For decorating supplies.

The Cake Craft Shop
www.cakecraftshop.co.uk
Tel: 01732 463573
Lots of lovely cookie cutters and
decorating supplies

**For more tips and advice on
making cookies, or to order
bespoke cookies and cakes for
special occasions, visit my
website www.chloecoker.com.**

acknowledgments

The past year has been an amazing experience, from
starting a small company to writing this book. None
of this would have been possible without some very
important people behind the scenes. With special
thanks to the following:

At Cico Books: to Cindy Richards for the opportunity, to
Sally Powell, Pete Jorgensen, Dawn Bates, and Alison Bolus
for their hard work in bringing this book to life, and to
Sonia Pugh and the sales and marketing team for getting
this book onto the shelves.

To Luis Peral for your beautiful styling and to Stuart
West, Martin Norris, and Emma Mitchell for your
fantastic photographs.

To Clare Young, for the inspiration for the gorgeous
Scandinavian birds, to Sophie Lourenco for sharing your
grandma's delicious recipe, and to Malcolm Billyard for
my lovely website.

To my fantastic family and team of cookie tasters, for
your love and support in whatever I choose to do and for
all the unusual cookie cutters you now collect for me. And
finally to my wonderful, and very patient, husband, Jon, for
encouraging me to take a risk, for allowing me to turn our
home into a cookie factory, and for your unquestioning
love, support, and humor, whatever time of day or night.